Adventures

in dining

Napa Valley

2003

by

Denise Schubert

GRAPEVINE PRESS, LLC
ST. HELENA, CA

Adventures in dining: Napa Valley 2003

Grapevine Press, LLC
P.O. Box 3554
Yountville, CA 94599
(707) 967-1073
custservice@adventuresindining.com
Website: www.adventuresindining.com

First Edition, January 2003
Second Printing, June 2003
ISBN 0-9723580-0-5

Cover Design by Dynamo Designs, New York City
Illustrations by Clay Seibert, San Francisco
Maps and Layout Design by Becki Haddad, Napa
Edited by Donna Leverenz, Calistoga

Author:
Denise Schubert

Although the author and publisher have made every effort to provide accurate, up-to-date information at press time, they accept no responsibility for loss, injury, or inconvenience sustained by any person using this book. Please be aware that hours of operation, menus and prices are subject to change, and restaurants may close without warning.

Table of Contents

Introduction

The idea behind *Adventures in dining* is very simple: There's nothing like visiting a special place with someone who actually lives there. Many people visit Napa Valley as much for the food as the wine so why not make dining part of the adventure? The author lives in St. Helena and looks forward to showing you around. She'll take you to all her favorite places, hot spots, and little-known gems. With *Adventures in dining* as your road map, you'll see the *real* Napa Valley from the locals' perspective, and you won't have to spend a fortune if you don't want to!

Adventures in dining is designed to be a constant companion, fitting easily into a glove compartment or purse. It is arranged by chapters, geographically rather than alphabetically, beginning with Napa and then traveling up valley through Yountville, Oakville, Rutherford, St. Helena and Calistoga. Each chapter is completely self-contained, beginning with a brief description of the town and a detailed map and key.

That's where the fun begins. *Adventures in dining* is not just about restaurants. You'll also learn where to go for an early morning latté, an ice cream cone, a late night snack, pizza, or a fabulous burger. If picnicking isn't on your agenda, it should be! World-class dining in Napa Valley isn't limited to fancy restaurants. Head to one of the many gourmet markets and put together your own feast, then let *Adventures in dining* lead you to a picnic spot with a world-class view. For a special treat, visit one of the local farmers markets and experience the good life that makes living here so special. Be sure to check out the "Hot Tip" at the bottom of each page designated by a chili pepper. This can be a tip on dining without a reservation, a recommended activity, a nearby attraction, or an interesting fact.

If you've still got energy to burn in the evening, let *Adventures in dining* be your guide to Napa Valley night life. This may seem like an oxymoron, and admittedly, Napa Valley is in no immediate danger of being called "the valley that never sleeps." But, believe it or not, there *is* life after 9pm. The streets may look like they've been rolled up, but *Adventures in dining* will show you where these night spots are hidden.

Criteria for inclusion in this book are based solely upon the opinions of the author who is an ardent diner and traveler, but *not* a food critic. If something is included it means the author likes the place, goes there frequently and recommends it to friends. It's all about having fun and trying new things. No compensation of any kind was received by the author or publisher in return for being included. In fact, most of the establishments had no idea a book was being written. Comments and suggestions are welcome and can be emailed to custservice@adventuresindining.com or mailed to Grapevine Press LLC, P.O. Box 3554, Yountville, CA 94599.

Bon appetit and many happy adventures!

Denise Schubert

Key to Maps, Symbols and Index

Adventures in dining explores Napa Valley town by town beginning with Napa at the southern end, then traveling upvalley through Yountville, Oakville, Rutherford, St. Helena and Calistoga. Each chapter is self-contained beginning with a brief introduction, map and location key, followed by dozens of recommended restaurants, delis, specialty markets, bakeries, espresso bars, ice cream parlors, farmers markets and picnic spots, as well as "nite" life activities.

MAPS: Keep in mind that maps are NOT drawn to scale. Areas have been expanded or compressed as needed to give you the best possible overview of the area while pinpointing the exact location.

SYMBOLS:

Full Bar

Wine & Beer

Outdoor Dining

Views & Vistas

CREDIT CARDS:

V – Visa

MC – Mastercard

AE – American Express

DC – Diners Club

HOT TIP: These little bits of information at the bottom of each page may be specific to the entry, or refer to a nearby attraction or related activity.

INDEX: Adventures in dining takes all the guesswork out of planning the perfect outing. Check the index at the back of the book to quickly find the spot that suits your mood. If you're looking for a killer view, a great burger, an ice cream cone, a romantic setting or a place still serving lunch at 3pm, you'll find it here. Index categories include:

- Views
- Delis
- Full Bar
- Ice Cream
- Nite Life

- Types of Cuisine
- Outdoor Dining
- Specialty Markets
- Farmers Markets
- Romantic Spots

Hamburgers or Pizza: Restaurants in all price ranges that regularly include hamburgers or pizza on the menu.

Espresso: Espresso drinks are available for takeout.

Late Kitchen: Places serving food until 10:30pm or later.

Continuous Dining: Food is served continuously during hours of operation.

Family Friendly: Families will feel welcome. The menu has selections suited to children.

Wine Bar: Specialty bars that offer a large selection of wines by the glass. Diners and non-diners are welcome.

Winning Wine List: Places that have an exceptional or unique wine list. This is not based solely on the number of selections.

Bay Area Top 100: The restaurant has appeared on at least one of the "top" lists put out by various magazines, radio stations and newspapers in the area.

Locals' Favorites: These are our personal favorites. Many are places that only locals would be able to tell you about.

Special Events or Private Parties: Accommodations can be made for special events and parties. Many have private rooms.

Catering: Catering services are available outside the restaurant.

Takeout: <u>Restaurants</u> with a takeout option. For additional takeout resources be sure to check delis and specialty markets.

Corkage Fees

Nearly all Napa Valley restaurants allow diners to bring in their own wine. Corkage fees vary widely and are per *each* 750ml bottle (a magnum will incur a two bottle fee). One corkage fee is often waived for each bottle purchased and some restaurants waive the corkage fee for locals, so be sure to ask.

Picnic Etiquette

We have included a great many wineries in our picnic sections for each chapter. It is always a good idea to call ahead and make sure the site is available that day. Most wineries do not require reservations, but many will reserve a table for you if they know when you are coming. While there is no charge for using these facilities, two simple rules of etiquette should be observed:

1. Always buy wine from the host winery.

2. As a courtesy, check in with the tasting room when you arrive. They like to know when the area is being used.

Napa

Cole's Chop House

Napa

The City of Napa has long been the "Rodney Dangerfield" of Napa Valley. Stop in Napa? People would actually "harumph" at the idea. Well, here's a news flash: If you thought the only reason to stop in Napa was to fill up the tank, think again.

A Wine Country-induced Renaissance is underway, with most of the activity centered squarely downtown, along the Napa River. At the south end of Main Street you'll find the recently restored Napa Mill complex, consisting of the A. Hatt building and grain mill, circa 1884. This was the largest historic restoration project ever undertaken in Napa and is now on the National Registry of Historic Landmarks. These distinguished brick buildings are now home to a luxury hotel, two restaurants, a specialty market, a bakery and several artists' studios.

The Napa Mill project is just one step in the City's ambitious long-range plan to make the riverfront a thriving commercial and cultural center with promenades, shops and restaurants. Two other riverfront projects were also completed recently: The ultra-modern American Center for Wine, Food and the Arts (COPIA) opened in November 2001 and the magnificent Napa Valley Opera House, a National Historic Landmark, reopened in June 2002. Further validation of renewed interest in downtown Napa was evidenced by the Napa Valley Repertory Theater performing its 2002 inaugural season at Native Sons of the Golden West Hall on Coombs Street, and the popular Napa Valley Shakespeare Festival relocating to Napa Mill's Riverfront Plaza in July 2002.

And as for the river itself, thanks to a $170 million flood abatement project, an enormous wetlands restoration and preservation project is underway that connects the wetlands of Napa all the way to San Pablo Bay. For a unique experience, rent a kayak from Napa River Adventures (707-224-9080) and see what's happening for yourself. You'll be amazed at the wealth of wildlife along the river including osprey, great blue herons, green herons, and if you're lucky, eagles and otters. Or for a truly romantic adventure, glide down the river in an authentic Venetian Gondola, courtesy of Gondola Servizio (707-257-8495).

Given all this activity, Napa's cuisine scene is really cooking. Nearly half of the Napa entries in this book are less than five years old; 15 have opened in the last year alone. You'll find Napa offers more choices for "type" of cuisine than upvalley towns (Indian, Japanese, e.g.), and there are many more choices in the low to intermediate price range.

It's not easy for a city to reinvent itself, but that's exactly what this one is doing. Come have a look!

NAPA

GREATER NAPA KEY

DINING ADVENTURES   SEE PAGE

PICNIC SITES

POINTS OF INTEREST

NAPA

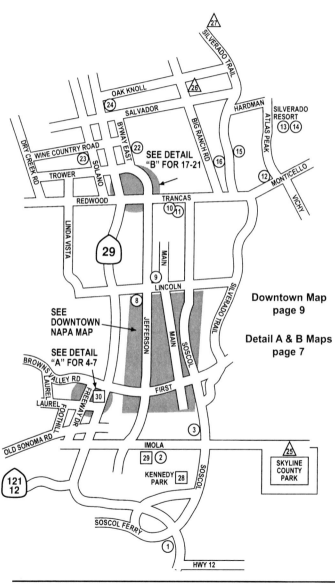

Downtown Map
page 9

Detail A & B Maps
page 7

SEE
DOWNTOWN
NAPA MAP

SEE DETAIL
"A" FOR 4-7

SEE DETAIL
"B" FOR 17-21

NAPA

GREATER NAPA DETAIL MAPS

⭕ **DINING ADVENTURES**   **SEE PAGE**

NAPA

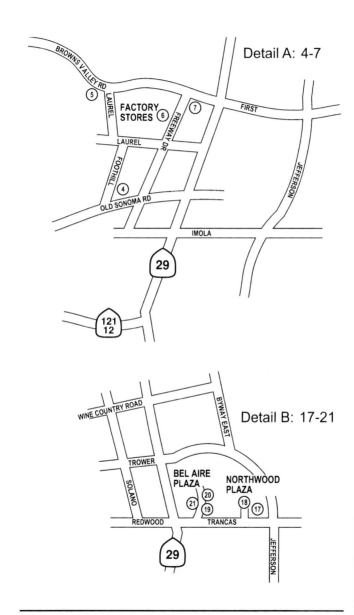

Detail A: 4-7

Detail B: 17-21

DOWNTOWN NAPA KEY

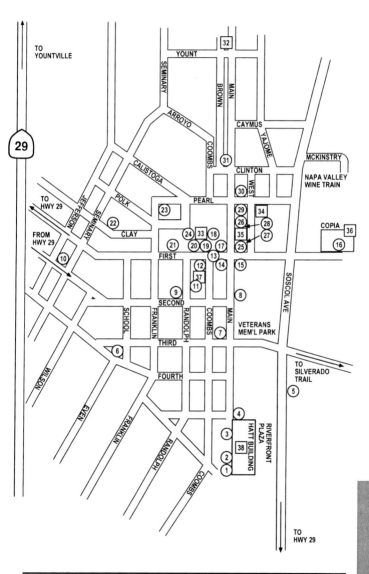

Notes

NAPA

ALEXIS BAKING COMPANY & CAFÉ (ABC)
1517 Third Street • Napa • (707) 258-1827

AMERICAN

ABC is a fantastic bakery that also happens to serve breakfast and lunch. Located in downtown Napa, in a boxy, nondescript building, it looks and feels like a hip 1960's diner: Counter service, Formica and chrome...you get the picture. The desserts are practically irresistible; in fact, NOT having dessert is a big mistake. The menus change daily and typically offer half a dozen choices. Espresso drinks are outstanding, and breakfast items often include several egg dishes, pancakes or French toast. Lunch is served from 11am until closing each day except Sunday, when it's breakfast only, from 11am-3pm. The uncomplicated menu is limited, but everything on it is very, very good. Lunch favorites include Chicken Caesar Salad, hamburgers, soups and sandwiches. Save room for dessert, or take one home. The cookies and brownies are great, but locals know that *ABC's* cakes are unbeatable: chocolate pound cake, apricot pistachio, carrot and chocolate caramel are regularly featured. Reservations are taken for parties of four or more.

OPEN DAILY
BREAKFAST:
M-F: 6:30am-11am
Sa: 8am-3pm
Su: 8am-2pm
Prices: $3-$6
LUNCH:
M-F: 11am-4pm
Sa: 11am-3pm
Prices: $4-$11

Espresso
Hamburgers
Sunday Brunch
Continuous Dining
No alcohol
Reservations: Yes

V, MC
Locals' Favorite
Family Friendly
Catering
Takeout
Chef / Owner:
Alexis Handleman

Have a special occasion coming up? ABC's famous for custom bakery work including birthday and wedding cakes.

NAPA

ANDIE'S CAFÉ
1042 Freeway Drive • Napa • (707) 259-1107

AMERICAN

CLOSED SUNDAYS

M-F: 7:30am-4pm
Sa: 8am-4pm

Espresso

Hamburgers: $5 & up

No Credit Cards

Family Friendly

Takeout

For those of you who like to shop the outlet stores AND have your car washed, THIS is the place to have a quick lunch. It also happens to make one of the best hamburgers in the valley! This tiny restaurant has been here for over five years and is definitely a local secret. If you drive by too fast on your way to the outlet stores, you won't even notice it. Look for the car wash located right next door, drop off your car and step into the café. By the time you are through eating, your car will be ready and you can begin your shopping across the street at the Napa Outlet Stores. If hamburgers don't sound good to you, try the portabella burger for $4.99, a BLT for $3.99, or perhaps a taco for $3.89. The best deal is the hamburger, fries and drink special for $6.19 Nice thick milkshakes are a meal in themselves. Self-service is the name of the game here, but the cooks are friendly and happy to customize your order. Espresso drinks are also available.

What a wonderful way to multi-task! Have a great hamburger lunch while watching your car get washed and planning your shopping spree.

NAPA

ANGÈLE

540 Main Street • Napa • (707) 252-8115

FRENCH

Angèle is the new kid on the block, opening just days before this book went to press. We decided to include it after just one dining experience because we were so impressed with the French-inspired menu, as well as the background and experience of the owners. *Angèle* is the newest venture of the Rouas family, with Claude, Bettina and Claudia as partners. Individually their resumes are impressive; together they are awesome. Claude's ventures have included *Auberge du Soleil*, *L'Etoile*, *Piatti* and San Ysido Ranch. Claude's daughter Bettina runs the show at *Angèle*, having honed her management skills at the *French Laundry*, *Bistro Jeanty* and *Bistro Don Giovanni* before realizing the dream of her own restaurant. *Angèle* is named after a neighborhood restaurant Bettina dearly loved when living in France. It was also her grandmother's name. Now *those* are good vibes. With dishes like Wild Mushroom Risotto, Roasted Black Sea Bass, and Veal Stew, we think there's a treat in store for all of us!

OPEN DAILY
11:30am-10pm

Moderately Priced
Lunch: approx $25

Continuous Dining
Wine Bar
Corkage: $15
Reservations: Yes

River View

V, MC, AE

Special Events

Chef:
Cristophe Gerard

Angèle is a great pre-theater spot! It's in the Hatt Mill complex, just a few blocks away from the Native Sons of the Golden West Hall, venue for the Napa Valley Repertory Theater.

NAPA

BELLE ARTI TRATTORIA SICILIANA
1040 Main Street • Napa • (707) 255-0720

ITALIAN

CLOSED SUNDAYS
LUNCH:
11:30am-2:30pm
Appetizers: $5-$8
Entrées: $8-$13
Desserts: $5.50

DINNER:
5:30pm-10pm
Appetizers: $6-$10
Entrées: $10-$24
Desserts: $5.50

Corkage: $10
Reservations: No

V, MC, AE
Special Events
Catering
Takeout

Chef: Rosario Patti

Santi Sacca and Rosario Patti felt compelled to open *Belle Arti* on September 11, 2002, as an emotional and symbolic gesture. Just weeks before that fateful day in 2001, the two men had opened their new restaurant across the river from the WTC, in the shadow of the Brooklyn Bridge. They, like many other business owners, lost everything in the economic aftermath of that tragic day. Months later, their friend and new partner, Russell Kassman, finally convinced them to move to Napa. *Belle Arti* is a fresh beginning, in a new town.

Located in the space formerly occupied by *Celadon*, the cozy look of this small eatery is relatively unchanged, with an open kitchen, comfortable table seating, bar seating for six, and a small outdoor deck. The food is fresh and flavorful and decidedly Sicilian, with seafood figuring prominently in the appetizers, pasta dishes, and main courses. Try the whole-roasted fish boned tableside. The moderately priced wine list is split between Sicilian and California offerings. Welcome to Napa, *Belle Arti* and Salute!

You're probably wondering what's with the Belle Arti logo: It's a whimsical combination of the two symbols of Sicily, the Medusa and the cactus pear. Mystery solved.

ADVENTURES IN DINING

NAPA

BISTRO DON GIOVANNI
4110 St. Helena Highway • Napa • (707) 224-3300

ITALIAN

Don Giovanni is consistently among the top-rated restaurants in the Bay Area. Located on the north side of Napa, just off Highway 29, it's easy to miss as you're headed up valley. Add this delightful spot to the DO NOT MISS list. Relax with the locals and enjoy the lively ambience either outside on the covered patio or inside this Tuscan-inspired restaurant. Husband and wife team Donna and Giovanni Scala make you feel right at home with their homemade pastas and breads. The wood-burning oven turns out thin crusted pizzas, while the mesquite grill does wonders with fresh vegetables, fish and meats. The beet and haricot vert salad is always a favorite starter, but it is hard to find a dish you won't like here. The portions are large, fresh and filled with flavor. Dessert is typically Italian. Try the tiramisu or granita with an espresso for a delicious ending to a great meal!

OPEN DAILY
LUNCH:
11:30am-5pm
DINNER:
Su-Th: 5pm-10pm
F-Sa: 5pm-11pm

Appetizers: $7-$9
Entrées: $12-$24
Desserts: $6

Pizza
Continuous Dining
Late Kitchen
Winning Wine List
Corkage: $15
Reservations: Yes

V, MC, AE, DC
Locals' Favorite
Bay Area Top 100
Special Events
Takeout

Chef: Scott Warner

Scott Warner from Rose Pistola in San Francisco is the new executive chef and is making owner Donna Scala very happy with his new creations.

NAPA

BOMBAY BISTRO
1106 First Street • Napa • (707) 253-9375

INDIAN

CLOSED SUNDAYS

LUNCH:
M-F: 11:30am-2pm
DINNER:
M-Sa: 5:30pm-9pm

Appetizers: $6-$13
Entrées: $10-$15
Desserts: $3-$5

Wine Shop
Winning Wine List
Corkage: $10
Reservations: Yes

V, MC, AE
Special Events
Catering
Takeout

Ethnic restaurants are something of a rarity in Napa Valley, so *Bombay Bistro* is a welcome addition. Bright and modern with high ceilings and curry-colored walls, an enormous stainless steel counter separates the large dining room from the kitchen. The three co-owners are from different parts of India, where the food varies greatly, region to region. *Bombay Bistro* offers authentic Indian specialties from all major regions, prepared in a "lighter and healthier" way. We found the dipping sauces to be surprisingly light and flavorful. Tandoori fans will be delighted to find lamb, chicken, poultry and fish on the menu, and vegetarians will appreciate the large number of meatless offerings. The appetizer sampler, which easily serves two to three ($12.95), or the dinner tasting menu for two ($29.75) are good ways to experiment. Some dishes have a 20-minute preparation time, so ask if you're on a schedule. An excellent 200+ wine list features a nice selection of California wines and some unusual Bordeaux and Burgundies that go nicely with the intense flavors of the food.

The owners' superb wine shop, Cork, adjoins the restaurant. Buy a bottle that's NOT on Bistro's wine list and have it with your meal with no corkage fee!

ADVENTURES IN DINING

NAPA

CAFÉ LUCY LE PETIT BISTRO
1408 Clay Street • Napa • (707) 255-0110

FRENCH

Lucy's definition of café as "a small, unpretentious, addictive restaurant" fits this charming bistro to a tee, making it a favorite hangout for people in the food business and locals alike. The ambience and food are inspired by the owners' frequent visits to their favorite bistros in France. A wisteria-covered patio, white lace curtains and colorful oilcloth tablecloths are the extent of the decoration, belying the complex and satisfying cuisine. Fabulous salads, sandwiches and "small plates" are perfect for sharing or lighter appetites. *Café Lucy's* rustic simplicity works even better at night, when romantic candlelight does wonders. Dinner entrées include pan-seared New York steak, herb-roasted chicken and petrale sole encrusted in cornmeal with lemon caper sauce. Many of the organic flowers, vegetables and herbs are from their own gardens. The attentive staff sees to your every need with genuine warmth. The exceptional wine list features over 100 wines from around the world.

CLOSED SUNDAYS
LUNCH:
M-Sa: 11am-3pm

DINNER Th-F only:
5:30pm-9:30pm

Appetizers: $5-$8
Entrées: $12-$18
Desserts: $4-$7

Winning Wine List
Corkage: $10
Reservations: Yes

V, MC, AE, DC
Locals' Favorite
Takeout

Chef: Lucy Gore

On Saturdays, Café Lucy is not open for dinner. Instead, the lunch menu is expanded to resemble a European-style midday meal. Lingering over coffee and dessert is mandatory.

CELADON

500 Main Street • Napa • (707) 254-9690

FUSION

OPEN DAILY

LUNCH:
11:30am-2:30pm
Appetizers: $5-$11
Entrées: $10-$23
Desserts: $4-$6

DINNER:
Su-Th: 5:30pm-9pm
F-Sa: 5:30pm-10pm
Appetizers: $5-$11
Entrées: $16-$23
Desserts: $4-$6

Corkage: $15
Reservations: Yes
(Dinner only)

V, MC, AE, DC
Locals' Favorite
Special Events
Catering

Chef / Owner:
Greg Cole

When Executive Chef/owner Greg Cole opened *Celadon* in late 1996, the wildly enthusiastic response sparked a "restaurant renaissance" in downtown Napa. Once again, Greg's on the cutting edge, relocating *Celadon* to the newly restored Hatt Building at the southern end of Main Street. Here, on the banks of the Napa River, a major transformation is underway, with chic new hotels and top-notch eateries locating along the River Walk. The new digs are very spacious, with wonderful al fresco dining, plus a good size bar area. The enormous landscaped terrace is fabulous at night (twinkle lights and heaters), and just steps away from Riverfront Plaza. Cole characterizes his cuisine as "global comfort food," featuring crab cakes, flash-fried calamari, seared ahi, and a 21-day dry-aged steak with pomme frites. It's a terrific lunch spot: salads, "small plates," and sandwiches are popular. *Celadon's* reasonably priced 100+ wine list includes 20 half-bottle selections, and a dozen wines by the glass.

The Napa Valley Shakespeare Festival performs around the corner in Riverfront Plaza Thursdays through Sundays, mid-July to mid-August. Call 1-800-965-4827 for tickets.

NAPA

COLE'S CHOP HOUSE

1122 Main Street • Napa • (707) 224-6328

AMERICAN

Imagine the 1950's and the wonderful steaks and chops you would find in the local restaurant complete with the mashed potatoes, creamed spinach, warm bread, etc…kick it up a notch…add an award-winning wine list, and you have the Napa Valley equivalent of the finest steak house north of San Francisco. The prices are not cheap, and everything is à la carte, but the quality of the prime-certified Angus beef dry-aged steaks define a new standard of excellence for a Napa Valley steak house. Located in the 114-year-old Williams-Kyser building with its vaulted ceilings, stone walls and polished fir floors, it is a treat to soak up local history while sipping classic cocktails at the bar or at your table. The visual effect of the restaurant is dramatic and quite stunning. If you want a more eclectic menu, check out Cole's other award-winning restaurant, *Celadon*, now located in the historic Hatt Building just a few blocks away.

CLOSED MONDAYS

DINNER:
Su,Tu-Th: 5pm-9pm
F-Sa: 5pm-10pm

Appetizers: $7-$9
Entrées: $17-$38
Sides: $4-$7
Desserts: $7-$9

Winning Wine List
Corkage: $15
Reservations: Yes

V, MC, AE

Special Events

Chef / Owner:
Greg Cole

Just south of Cole's is the beautifully restored Napa Valley Opera House, which reopened in June of 2002. It is a gem! Check the marquee for events.

DEPOT

806 Fourth Street • Napa • (707) 252-4477

ITALIAN

CLOSED MON-TUES

HOURS:
W-Sa: 5pm-9:30pm
Su: 2pm-9pm

3-course dinners:
$15-$21
À la carte Entrées:
$13-$19
Desserts: $5-$6

Corkage: $3/person
Reservations: Yes

V, MC
Locals' Favorite
Family Friendly
Special Events
Catering
Takeout

Chef:
Clemente Cittoni

Locals have been flocking to the family-run *Depot* to celebrate birthdays, anniversaries, and good friends for 30 years. You have to be looking for it: it's located at the north end of a used car lot on Soscol. No attitudes, soft music or candlelight here; just wood floors, Formica tables, a deer head over the bar and great Italian food like you *wish* your Mamma made. Co-owner/chef Clemente Cittoni regularly greets customers with hugs all around, and every guest, old and new, is made to feel at home. It seems only fitting many of the dishes are served family style. The most famous is malfatti, a delicious concoction of spinach, onion, garlic, egg, cheese and pesto, rolled and then poached. Served smothered in red sauce, you'd swear you were eating little sausages, but it is entirely meatless. This famous recipe was created in 1925 when the original owner of the Depot Hotel was trying to make ravioli but had no pasta dough. Using just the filling, she improvised. "Malfatti" may be Italian for "mistake," but it's our good fortune!

The ultimate takeout: Bring your own pot to the Depot's back door, and they'll fill it with malfatti for you to take home.

ADVENTURES IN DINING

FOOTHILL CAFÉ
2766 Old Sonoma Road • Napa • (707) 252-6178

CALIFORNIA

Foothill Café is definitely a favorite of the local population, and until recently, they were the only ones able to find it! After the *Chronicle* named it as one of the Top 100 Bay Area Restaurants several years ago, many visitors have found their way to this little strip mall on the east side of Napa. Reservations are a must with seating limited to 42. There is no bar or waiting area, but *Foothill* has prompt seating down to a science. Brightly painted yellow walls hung with local artwork and signs designed to make you chuckle create a happy ambience and express the whimsical nature of owner/chef Jerry Shaffer, formerly of *Masa's* in San Francisco. Baby back ribs from the wood burning oven are a menu staple and always terrific, but the nightly specials are guaranteed to get your attention, not to mention fabulous side orders like potatoes au gratin made with Stilton cheese! Since winemakers and chefs love to come here, it is no wonder the wine list is full of good choices. Desserts are delicious!

CLOSED MON-TUES

DINNER:
4:30pm-9:30pm
Appetizers: $6-$7
Entrées: $11-$15
Desserts:$5

Winning Wine List
Corkage: $10
Reservations: Yes

V, MC, AE, DC
Locals' Favorite
Bay Area Top 100
Special Events
Catering
Takeout

Chef: Jerry Shaffer

Old Sonoma Road is located between the First Street and Imola exits off Hwy 29. Take Freeway Drive and turn on Old Sonoma Road. Go to Foothill Blvd: the café will be on the right.

NAPA

FUJIYA
921 Factory Stores Drive • Napa • (707) 257-0639

JAPANESE

CLOSED MONDAYS

LUNCH:
11:30am-2pm
DINNER:
5pm-9:30pm

Appetizers: $4-$10
Entrées: $14-$23
Desserts: $4-$5

Corkage: $4.75
Reservations: Yes

Wine • Beer • Sake

V, MC

Special Events

Takeout

The Napa Premium Outlet Shopping Center is an unlikely location for a Japanese restaurant, and believe it or not, *Fujiya* was there first. Located near the north end of the mall, it's so understated as to be nearly invisible. The waitresses' pretty "California-style" kimonos and bartender's black tie add some panache to the simple décor. There is a 6-seat sushi bar and a private screened area that comfortably accommodates 8-10, with traditional tatami seating (low tables with cushions). The widely spaced tables are conducive to serious conversation, a welcome change from most restaurants. Though not inexpensive, entrées include miso soup, salad and rice, and food quality compares favorably to Japanese restaurants in the City. The extensive menu includes many innovative roll combinations, gyoza, sushi, sashimi, light-as-a-feather Tempura, and nicely balanced Teriyaki dishes. The wine selection is very limited, but there is a good selection of beer and sake.

There is a free Trolley Car that runs from the Premium Outlet Center to downtown Napa, continuing to COPIA, every half hour.

NAPA

FUMÉ BISTRO
4050 Byway East • Napa • (707) 257-1999

CALIFORNIA

Opening in 2002 to rave reviews, owners Terry and Gigi Letson successfully created a neighborhood restaurant geared to the Napa Valley community of diners. The elegant, understated décor works equally well with casual and more intimate dining experiences. Tables are not set too close together and are conducive to private conversation. Entrées reflect the tastes acquired from years of international travel, although most dishes find their origin in France. Like most good restaurants in the Napa Valley, Terry makes good use of the freshest ingredients available and changes the menu often to reflect the season's best offerings. Families with young children can feel comfortable here. A "Little Ones Menu" offers several complete meals for just $7.50. If you're after a great martini or a terrific burger, step up to the bar and enjoy the talents of Andrew Geuercio. You'll have no trouble finding the perfect bottle of wine from the extensive wine list.

CLOSED TUESDAYS

HOURS:
Su-M, W-Th:
4:30pm-10pm
F-Sa: 4:30pm-11pm

Appetizers: $6-$9
Entrées: $10-$20
Desserts: $5-$7

Hamburgers
Pizza
Late Kitchen (F-Sa)
Winning Wine List
Corkage: $10
Reservations: Yes

V, MC, AE
Locals' Favorite
Family Friendly
Special Events
Catering
Takeout

Chef: Terry Letson

Fumé Bistro has a very attractive bar and an excellent bartender. For an exotic start to your meal, ask for a Plantation Mojito.

GILLWOOD'S CAFÉ & BAKERY
1320 Napa Town Center • Napa • (707) 253-0409

AMERICAN

OPEN DAILY

BREAKFAST:
8am-3pm
Prices: $4-$9

LUNCH:
10:30am-3pm
Prices: $4-$10
Desserts: $3-$4

Hamburgers
Continuous Dining
No Alcohol
Reservations: No

V, MC

Locals Favorite

Family Friendly

Takeout

Located in the outdoor shopping mall called Napa Town Center, *Gillwood's* offers a full breakfast and lunch menu identical to its sister restaurant in St. Helena. Service is always fast and friendly, and the atmosphere is casual and pleasant. Trademark scrambles, breakfast platters, omelets, Belgian waffles and French toast are served until 3pm daily. Homemade soups, salads, and sandwiches make this a popular luncheon spot for business people and shoppers on the go. What differentiates the Napa location from upvalley is its onsite bakery and outdoor patio on the mall courtyard. There's no real view, but it's ideal for people watching. The bakery isn't large by any means, but many of the bakery items are unique to *Gillwood's* and are truly outstanding. The raspberry streusel muffin and the lemon or orange mini-bundt cakes are major standouts.

Looking for info about wineries, lodging and activities? The Napa Valley Visitors Center is next door. However, it's scheduled to move to the Hatt Building, 500 Main, early in 2003.

JULIA'S KITCHEN • AMERICAN MARKET CAFÉ
COPIA • 500 First Street • Napa • (707) 265-5700

FRENCH

New in November of 2001 and named for Julia Child, advisor and Honorary Trustee of COPIA, *Julia's Kitchen* is centrally located on COPIA's main floor. Dining is a learning experience here, with a wide-open dining room designed for watching the chefs at work in the dramatic open kitchen. Casually watch the chefs prepare your food from a distance, or order the 5-course Chef's Tasting Menu ($65) and sit at the coveted Kitchen Table for a closer look. Chef Mark Dommen creates French-inspired dishes without the cream and butter base of traditional dishes; many of the ingredients come from the surrounding gardens.

For an informal and less expensive meal, visit the *American Market Café*, a deli-style eatery featuring delicious prepared foods. Eat outside on the patio surrounded by olive trees and lovely gardens. COPIA has a non-stop schedule of food and wine related activities and classes: Every Monday, food and wine pairing classes include a light lunch. Visit www.copia.org for a complete schedule of upcoming activities.

WINTER 10/1-2/28
Lunch: Th-Mon
11:30am-3pm
Dinner: Fri-Sat
5:30pm-9:30pm
SUMMER 3/1-9/31
Lunch: Wed-Mon
11:30am-3pm
Dinner: Th-Su
5:30pm-9:30pm
Appetizers: $9-$18
Entrées: $20-$30
Desserts: $8

Corkage: $15
Reservations: Yes
V, MC, AE
Special Events
Catering
Chef: Mark Dommen

AMERICAN CAFÉ
10/1-2/28:
Th-Mon:10am-5pm
3/1-9/31:
Wed-Mon: 10am-5pm

Esquire Magazine named Julia's Kitchen "Restaurant of the Year" for 2002. Julia Child's famous collection of copper cookware is now part of COPIA's core exhibition!

NAPA

LA BOUCANE

1778 Second Street • Napa • (707) 253-1177

FRENCH

CLOSED SUNDAYS

DINNER:
5:30pm-10:30pm

Appetizers: $5-$8
Entrées: $15-$22
Desserts: $7

Corkage: $15
Reservations: Yes

V, MC

Romantic Spot

Special Events

Chef:
Jacques Mokrani

When you are in the mood for romance and a nice quiet evening, make a reservation here and plan on stepping back in time. Chef Jacques Mokrani serves traditional dishes found in the best French restaurants thirty years ago and makes no apologies for using lots of butter and cream in the sauces. Julia Child would love it here! Butter lettuce salad with an herbed vinaigrette and mushrooms is simple and elegant and a refreshing change from the mesclun so common today. Creamed spinach is a staple and works well with the sautéed chicken or roasted lamb entrées. Of course soufflés and mousses make an appearance on the dessert menu. The wine list has been chosen to match the hearty dishes, with a good selection at a variety of prices. The ambience of this restored Victorian home with its wallpapered walls, ornate moldings, high ceilings, plenty of candles and flowers goes perfectly with the classic style of French cuisine. *La Boucane* is the ideal antidote for a "hurry-up" day.

Napa has several residential neighborhoods with historical landmark status that are well worth visiting. This is the only restaurant located in one of these wonderful Victorian buildings!

ADVENTURES IN DINING

NAPA

MISTO

916 Franklin Street • Napa * (707) 252-4080

ITALIAN

In the world of makeovers, this one gets an A+. *Misto* exchanged the very casual café look for starched linens, soft lighting, grape motif murals, and textured walls for a more elegant Tuscan look. Locals love the teddy-bear charisma of owner/chef Tom Wagstaff who makes certain *Misto* remains a friendly and unpretentious place, practically insured by the white butcher paper and crayons on each table. The long, narrow dining area is dominated by the attractive wine bar lining one side. When crowded, the decibel level can be pretty high. The menu regularly features Italian "comfort food" such as risotto, spaghetti, osso bucco, veal scaloppine, and Sonoma duck, as well as seasonal specials of fresh fish, shellfish, and local produce. The wine list offers a very good selection of over 100 Californian (primarily Napa) and Italian wines in all price ranges, with over 30 wines by the glass.

OPEN DAILY
LUNCH:
M-F: 11:30am-2pm
Appetizers: $3-$10
Entrées: $9-$14
Desserts: $5-$7

DINNER:
S-Th: 5pm-9pm
F-Sa: 5pm-10pm
Appetizers: $4-$12
Entrées: $13-$26
Desserts: $5-$7

Wine Bar
Winning Wine List
Corkage: $10
Reservations: Yes

V, MC, AE, DC
Locals' Favorite
Special Events
Catering
Takeout

Chef: Tom Wagstaff

Misto has one of Napa's best wine bars, offering extensive (and reasonable) selections by the glass. No dinner reservations? Try snagging a seat at the Wine Bar.

NAPA

PAIRS

4175 Solano Avenue • Napa • (707) 224-8464

FUSION

OPEN DAILY
LUNCH:
11:30am-9:30pm
Prices: $9-$12
Desserts: $7

DINNER:
5:30pm-10:30pm
Appetizers: $6-$12
Entrées: $16-$26
Desserts: $7

Continuous Dining
Late Kitchen
Wine, Beer, Sake
Corkage: $15
Reservations: Yes

V, MC, AE
Locals' Favorite
Family Friendly
Special Events
Catering
Takeout

Chef: Craig Schauffel

The first thing you notice about this restaurant is the tranquil décor and its Zen-like atmosphere. Bamboo screens at the entryway, soft lighting and neutral colors perfectly complement the unique wine and sake bar. Clearly the centerpiece of the room, the bar is constructed from a single piece of curved, highly polished wood set on a base of native river rocks. This is just the place to try one of the "sake cocktails" for a new taste treat! Subtle Asian influences are evident in nearly all the most popular dishes including Roasted Mussels in Coconut Broth, Crispy Calamari with Lemon and Fennel, and Lemon Glazed Chicken. Here's another nice touch unique to *Pairs*: The chefs always look past the food to the wine, so, when you look at the menu, every item is accompanied by a particular wine recommendation–hence the name "*Pairs*." In fact, the entire wine list is a reflection of what the chefs believe will best enhance their menu, including a very nice selection of Reserve wines for those special occasions.

Pairs offers a special childrens' menu ranging from $6-$10, and even has a Cigar Menu starting at $15! And if you need catering, Pairs is top-notch.

PEARL

1339 Pearl Street • Napa • (707) 224-9161

CALIFORNIA

Pearl is located in the heart of downtown, but away from the storefronts of First Street. Decorated in warm and creamy colors, with only eleven lacquered pine tables and a counter area with six metal stools, the dining experience is intimate but unimposing. Vaulted ceilings and exposed wood are accented by sculpture, artwork and pottery by local artists giving added dimension to the lovely dining room. The patio is a pleasant option in nice weather. We love the colorful Hex Signs on the walls created by Kathy Dennett (which can be made to order). Years ago, co-owner Nikkie Zeller worked at *The Diner* in Yountville, so the eclectic and inspired menu comes as no surprise. Daily choices may include Hog Island oysters, crab cakes, flank steak tacos, or lamb shank braised Moroccan style. Grab one of *Pearl's* coveted counter seats to get a bird's-eye view of talented Chef Jose Bravo at work in the kitchen. At least 10 wines are offered by the glass, and the wine list features carefully selected and nicely priced California and international wines.

CLOSED SUN-MON

LUNCH:
11:30am-2pm
DINNER:
5:30pm-9:30pm

Appetizers: $6-$15
Entrées: $9-$20
Desserts: $5-$7

Corkage: $12
Reservations: Yes

V, MC
Locals' Favorite
Special Events
Catering
Takeout

Chef: Jose Bravo

Owners:
Nikkie & Pete Zeller

Half of each corkage fee goes to the local humane society. As a result, Pearl is one of their largest benefactors, happily contributing thousands of dollars each year!

NAPA

PICCOLINO'S ITALIAN CAFÉ
1385 Napa Town Center • Napa • (707) 251-0100

ITALIAN

OPEN DAILY

LUNCH / DINNER:
11am-9pm
Appetizers: $5-$10
Entrées: $11-$18
Desserts: $4-$6
Sunday Brunch
11am-3pm

Pizza
Wine Bar
Continuous Dining
Corkage: $8
Reservations: Yes

V, MC, AE, DC
Live Music (W, F, Sa)
Locals' Favorite
Family Friendly
Special Events
Takeout

Owner: Joe Salerno
Chef: Charles Trester

Located in Napa Town Center, *Piccolino's* is the kind of place that feels warm and comfortable the minute you walk in. There are two good-sized dining areas and a wine bar, plus an outdoor patio on the Town Center plaza. Paintings and murals of the Italian countryside decorate the walls and become the backdrop for roving owner Joe Salerno as he greets guests and works on making them happy ...just like the man in the 1940's song "Papa Piccolino." Let the heavenly smells of garlic bread and olive oil tickle your taste buds in anticipation of "Old World Italian Family Cooking." Ravioli, eggplant Parmesan, veal piccata, fettucini mare, and *Piccolino's* famous lasagna are just a few of the house specialties. Every Wednesday celebrates "Old Italy Night" with a special menu and Steve Albini singing Italian songs and playing his accordion. Singers and musicians also perform Friday and Saturday nights, adding to the fun. The wine list includes a good selection of California wines plus an unusual selection of Italian wines from Puglia and Sardinia.

Poppa's Family Size Dinners including a pasta dish, bread and salad, serve 4-5 hungry people for $33-$43. There is also a special Bambino menu kids will love.

ADVENTURES IN DINING

NAPA

PIZZA AZZURRO
1400 Second Street • Napa • (707) 255-5552

ITALIAN

Pizza Azzurro is a welcome addition to the Napa cuisine scene. There are few pizzerias of this calibre anywhere! The simple modern decor is bright and airy, thanks to floor-to-ceiling windows and a convenient corner location, just a block away from Napa Town Center. A pizza oven turns out terrific thin-crusted pizzas that go nicely with a variety of seasonal salads. Some say *Pizza Azzurra* makes the best Caesar salad in the valley! If pasta suits your fancy, choose from a baked rigatoni with sausage, or perhaps a vegetarian fusilli with zucchini, corn, spinach and lemon. There is a nice selection of moderately priced California wines, as well as locally made beers and sodas. The menu and moderate prices make this a popular spot with the younger set. Great for takeout or eating in.

CLOSED SUNDAYS

LUNCH / DINNER:
M-F: 11:30am-9pm
Sa: 5pm-10pm

Pizza: $9-$11

Pasta: $9-$12

Continuous Dining
Corkage: $10
Reservations: No

V, MC, AE

Family Friendly

Special Events

Catering

Takeout

Great location. One block from the Napa Town Center and the soon-to-reopen Uptown Theatre, and within easy walking distance of the Opera House and the Napa Riverfront!

NAPA

RED ROCK CAFÉ
1010 Lincoln Avenue • Napa • (707) 226-2633

AMERICAN

OPEN DAILY

HOURS:
Su-W: 11am-9:30pm
Th-Sa: 11am-10pm

Prices: $5-$10

Hamburgers
Microbrews

Continuous Dining
Corkage: $1
Reservations: No

V, MC, AE, DC
Locals' Favorite
Family Friendly
Catering
Takeout

If you're craving a fantastic hamburger, head to *Red Rock*, a favorite hole-in-the-wall on the corner of Lincoln and Main. Tiny, with not a speck of ambience, this neighborhood bar turns out thick, juicy burgers that are simply the best. The basic 1/3 pounder starts at $4.50, then add your choice of toppings including pepper jack, avocado, bacon, mushrooms, green peppers, olives, salsa, sautéed onions and BBQ sauce. A tasty Char Tri-Tip Sandwich and slow-roasted BBQ Pork Sandwich have been added to the menu thanks to their popular takeout facility in the back called *Back Door BBQ*. Huge baskets of French fries or onion rings easily serve two people. There's always a great selection of microbrews on tap and in bottles, plus a few wines by the glass. *Back Door BBQ* (takeout only) has expanded its "by-the-pound" menu beyond the Char Tri-Tip and slow-roasted pork to include baby back ribs, chicken, and a whole lotta fixin's. *Red Rock* has another location at 4084 Byway East, Napa.

Back Door BBQ takeout is available at the Lincoln location only. Call a different number, (707) 252-9250, to order; it's faster.

NAPA

RISTORANTE ALLEGRIA
1026 First Street • Napa • (707) 254-8006

ITALIAN

One of the newest additions to Napa's cuisine scene, *Ristorante Allegria* is housed in an old bank building saved from demolition in the early 1990's by Napa County Landmarks. Owners Baris and Rodi Yildiz spent months transforming raw space into a lovely restaurant with soaring 20-foot ceilings, crown moldings, creamy earth tones, soft lighting, white linens and Riedel glassware. We love the atmosphere, but it is very noisy. The restaurant and Wine Bar are open until 11pm daily, 11:30pm weekends, making *Ristorante Allegria* an ideal spot for a late meal or an after-theatre nightcap. Chef Ramiro Nolazco prepares his favorites from several regions, including northern Italian Risotto and the Roman specialty Saltimbocca. We've enjoyed our entrées on every visit, but found the appetizers (with the exception of the excellent mussels) to be hit or miss. The luncheon menu has a nice selection of sandwiches and salads. The 75+ wine list is reasonably priced; about half are Italian, half from Napa Valley.

OPEN DAILY

LUNCH: 11am-3pm
Appetizers: $7-$11
Entrées: $8-$19
Desserts: $4-$6

DINNER: 5pm-11pm
F-Sa: 5pm-11:30pm
Appetizers: $6-$14
Entrées: $11-$19
Desserts: $4-$6

Late Kitchen
Wine Bar
Corkage: $15
Reservations: Yes

V, MC, AE
Romantic Spot
Special Events
Catering

Chef:
Ramiro Nolazco

This lovely Classical Revival building originally housed the First National Bank (circa 1910) and is on the National Register of Historic Places.

NAPA

ROYAL OAK • SILVERADO RESORT
1600 Atlas Peak Road • Napa • (707) 257-0200

CALIFORNIA

OPEN DAILY

DINNER:
6pm-10:30pm
Appetizers: $6-$13
Entrées: $20-$35
Desserts: $7.50

Late Kitchen
Winning Wine List
Corkage: $15
Reservations: Yes

V, MC, AE, DC
Romantic Spot
Nite Life
Special Events
Catering

Chef: Peter Pahk

Between the gorgeous dark wood paneling and the great view overlooking the south golf course, the *Royal Oak* practically oozes charm and old-fashioned elegance. This signature restaurant of Silverado Resort is known for its beautifully presented mesquite grilled steaks, seafood, and poultry, prepared by award-winning chef, Peter Pahk. Hawaiian born and trained at the CIA in Hyde Park, Peter was Executive Sous Chef at the Ritz-Carlton Hotel Company for over ten years before joining Silverado in 1997. He is currently executive chef for all of the restaurants at the Resort. The menu features traditional favorites like Caesar Salad prepared tableside, and the colorful Jumbo Prawn Cocktail with Vegetable Confetti and Tomato Horseradish Sauce. Delicious side dishes such as Tian of Moussaka and crispy Risotto cake complement the entrées nicely. Pastry chef Ivan Rodriguez satisfies the sweet tooth with classic desserts including Baked Alaska and crème brulée.

Silverado Country Club and Resort is worth a visit in itself. Enjoy cocktails (11am-1am) and appetizers (11am-10pm) in front of the fireplace or on the patio of The Main Lounge Bar.

NAPA

SAKETINI ASIAN DINER & LOUNGE
3900 Bel Aire Plaza • Napa • (707) 255-7423

ASIAN

The cuisine at *Saketini* is nearly impossible to categorize because alongside the daily sushi and sashimi specials you'll find Tiger Shrimp with Thai Peanut Dipping Sauce, a Bay Shrimp Wonton Salad, PLUS a terrific BLT and hamburger! As scattered as this menu appears to be, it all seems to work. Marinades, ginger glazes, and pineapple honey BBQ sauce add a nice dimension to fresh seafood, pork ribs and beef. The food is consistently fresh and flavorful, and it's fun to have so many different choices when you're in the mood for Asian food.

The cavernous space next door to the restaurant is now the *Saketini Asian Lounge*. The term "Lounge" is used loosely -- it's really nothing more than four walls, cement floors, a large bar, and a few pieces of well-used furniture placed in front of a TV set. BUT... add a DJ and a dance floor and you've got a formula for success. It's a very popular place with the 20-and 30-something crowd, and it is PACKED on the weekends. See Napa Nite Life (p. 58) for more information.

OPEN DAILY

LUNCH:
M-Sa: 11:30am-2pm
DINNER:
5pm-9pm

Appetizers: $3-$9
Entrées: $8-$15
Desserts: $5-$7

Corkage: $7.50
Reservations: No

V, MC, AE, DC
Nite Life
Takeout

ASIAN LOUNGE
5pm-2am
May close earlier on
weekdays

Saketini's Asian Lounge is definitely THE hot spot in downtown Napa on weekends, open until 2am, with a DJ and dance floor.

NAPA

SUSHI MAMBO
1202 First Street • Napa • (707) 257-6604

JAPANESE

CLOSED SUNDAYS

LUNCH:
M-F: 11:45am-2pm
DINNER:
M-Sa: 5:30pm-9pm

Appetizers: $4-$9
Entrées: $8-$15
Desserts: $4-$6

Corkage: None
Reservations: Yes

Sake • Beer • Wine

V, MC, AE

Locals' Favorite

Family Friendly

Takeout

Sushi Mambo may be the only Japanese restaurant where the sushi chefs are from Mexico and trained in Japan. The casual, friendly atmosphere and great sushi have attracted a loyal following, particularly the downtown lunch crowd. Sushi rolls are unusually creative and delicious, with silly names like Rolling Blackout, Bubba Gump, and Rock 'n' Roll. The Nutty Professor with shrimp, crab, and macadamia nuts is one of our favorites. *Sushi Mambo* is located in the Old Napa Register Building. This lovely circa 1910 building is on the National Register of Historic Places and is one of the few historic buildings remaining in downtown Napa. The dining room is attractive and spacious, with additional seating at the sushi bar. Thanks to a new, improved kitchen, the menu has been expanded to include Teriyaki, Tempura, Katsu (breaded cutlets), Udon (noodles), Sukiyaki and Yosenabe (stew). There's a nice selection of Japanese and domestic beer, sake, and several wines.

Sushi Mambo is very kid friendly. We're always amazed at how many families we see with kids of all ages enjoying Japanese food!

ADVENTURES IN DINING

TUSCANY
1005 First Street • Napa • (707) 258-1000

ITALIAN

The architectural design of this corner ristorante is ingenious. The two walls fronting Main and First Streets are composed entirely of French doors, which can be folded back to varying degrees, giving the impression of a sidewalk cafe. The Tuscan influence is not only evident on the outside, it surrounds you on the inside as well, with subtle terra cotta colors, lovely wall murals, pale wood tables and floors and soft lighting. The beautiful dining room is large and open, with additional seating at a long counter facing the kitchen. Another equally pleasant seating option is in the bar "area" (the distinction between "bar" and "dining room" is more illusionary than real). All this is the perfect backdrop for the tantalizing aromas wafting from the kitchen and the wood-fired pizza oven. Soups, salads, pizza or perhaps a sandwich on warm foccacia bread are perfect for smaller appetites or at lunch. The dinner menu features creative pasta dishes, veal, chicken, pork, and beef. *Tuscany* does a superb job with fresh fish!

OPEN DAILY

LUNCH:
11:30am-2:30pm
Appetizers:$4-$14
Entrées: $6-$14
Desserts:$4-$6

DINNER:
5:30pm-10pm
Appetizers: $5-$11
Entrées: $14-$28
Desserts: $5-$7

Pizza
Corkage: $15
Reservations: Yes

V, MC, AE
Locals' Favorite
Special Events
Catering
Takeout
Chefs:
Mathew Newton
Marcos Garcia

Enjoy the lively atmosphere of this Tuscan venue with friends…the long table in back is perfect for a party of eight! Oh, and pay attention to the daily "specials," which really are!

NAPA

UVA TRATTORIA

1040 Clinton (at Brown) • Napa • (707) 255-6646

ITALIAN

CLOSED MONDAYS

HOURS:
Tu-F: 11:30am-10pm
Sa: 5pm-10pm
Su: 11am-9pm

Appetizers: $3-$9
Entrées: $9-$17
Desserts: $5-$6

Pizza
Continuous Dining
Wine Bar
Corkage: $10
Reservations: Yes

V, MC, AE
Nite Life
Locals' Favorite
Special Events
Takeout

Chef / Owner:
Sean Pramuk

Located a few blocks away from the heart of downtown Napa, *Uva* has been completely rejuvenated under new, energetic management. The service is crisp and attentive, and the food has never been better. The main dining room is really two adjoining rooms: a sunny, enclosed porch-like area fronts the street, with a larger dining area immediately behind. Traditional Italian favorites such as pizza, gnocchi, spaghetti carbonara, veal piccata and roasted chicken are all outstanding. Immediately to the right upon entering is the new enoteca, or food and wine tasting bar. Assaggini (little tastes) are served here until 10pm, and the owner hopes to expand these hours in the near future. "Little tastes" are $5-$8 and include, among other things, antipasto, calamari fritti, and cheeses. From the looks of things, locals have already discovered that *Uva* is ideal for large parties and special events. Just past the enoteca is a very versatile room that works well for one large group (up to 150) or several small groups.

The owner makes his own limoncino, a delicious liqueur. Ask him to pour you a glass after dinner.

ADVENTURES IN DINING

VILLA CORONA - NAPA
3614 Bel Aire Plaza • Napa • (707) 257-8685

MEXICAN

Some say the Mexican fare at this original location of *Villa Corona* is even better than its satellite in St. Helena. Frankly, we think they are both excellent. *Villa Corona* has been serving "authentic" Mexican food in Napa since 1983. Tucked away in the southeastern corner of the Bel Aire shopping center at California and Trancas, the restaurant's simple décor is dated and very basic. But never mind the ambience; the succulent carnitas, tender chile verde, hefty burritos, and spicy camarones (prawns) sauteed in garlic or hot sauce make the decorating irrelevant. And you won't find better enchiladas, flautas, or tamales. A good selection of Mexican and domestic bottled beers are available. Breakfast is served until 11am daily (closed Monday). Kick-start your day with the spicy huevos rancheros. Everything on the menu is available for takeout.

CLOSED MONDAYS

BREAKFAST:
Tu-Sa: 9am-11am
Su: 8am-11am

LUNCH / DINNER:
Tu-Sa: 11am-9pm
Su: 11am-8pm

Prices: $3-$11

Continuous Dining
Corkage: None
Reservations: No

V, MC

Locals' Favorite

Family Friendly

Catering

Takeout

On Saturday and Sunday, Villa Corona makes a delicious beef BBQ with rice and beans for $8.95, but call ahead to place your order; it sells out!

NAPA

VILLA ROMANO
1011 Soscol Ferry Road • Napa • (707) 252-4533

ITALIAN

OPEN DAILY

LUNCH:
M-F:11:30am-2:30pm
DINNER:
M-F: 5pm-9pm
Sa: 5pm-10pm
Su: 4pm-9pm

Appetizers: $4-$13
Entrées: $15-$21
Desserts: $5 -$7

Winning Wine List
Corkage: $13
Reservations: Yes

V, MC, AE, DC
Locals' Favorite
Special Events
Takeout

Chef / Owner:
Daniel Guillen

This little-known gem on the south side of Napa appears to be in the middle of nowhere, located on the southwest corner of the intersection of Hwy 29, Soscol Ferry Road and Napa-Vallejo Highway. Actually, it's very close to Napa's Industrial Park and is very popular for lunch. *Villa Romano* is the perfect choice if you got a late start for your weekend in the Napa Valley and need a cozy place to dine before heading upvalley or just if you're looking for a fun dining experience "off the beaten path." The quaint, 2-story farmhouse-turned-restaurant is owned by Chef Daniel Guillen, who began his career at *Auberge du Soleil* studying under Chef Masa Cobauchi for six years before opening *Villa Romano* in 1992. The menu of northern Italian dishes is extensive, divided into antipasti, salads, pastas, and entrées in the traditional Italian fashion. The fresh pastas are all homemade, elevating lasagna to gourmet status. With over 150 labels on the wine list, from all over the world in all price ranges, it is easy to find one you'll enjoy.

Special holiday and Monthly Winemaker Dinners feature an elegant 5-course meal, paired with the featured vintner's selections ($65 per person)!

VINTNERS COURT • BAR & GRILL
1600 Atlas Peak Road • Napa • (707) 257-0200

FUSION

Vintners Court, sister restaurant to the *Royal Oak* at Silverado Resort, serves dinner three times a week. Specializing in fish and seafood prepared with a Pacific Rim flair, the Friday Seafood Buffet has become a Napa Valley tradition. The impressive buffet, accented by tropical flowers and ice sculptures, features an endless parade of fresh fish and shellfish. Shrimp, salmon, calamari, mussels, and fresh sushi are just the "starters." Hawaiian swordfish, grilled mahi, braised clams and mussels, seared shark and Maine lobster share the "main course" spotlight. For those preferring something other than seafood, try the marinated chicken with lemongrass or slow-roasted prime rib. Thursday and Saturday night are à la carte, with table service.

Silverado's casual *Bar & Grill* is open daily featuring tradtional breakfast fare until 11:30am, then soups, salads and sandwiches until 6pm. Enjoy great views of the gardens and championship golf course.

VINTNERS COURT
Closed Dec-Mar
Th-Sa: 6pm-9:30pm
Appetizers: $11-$12
Entrées: $25-$32
Desserts: $8

Seafood Buffet $42

Winning Wine List
Corkage: $15
Reservations: Yes

V, MC, AE, DC
Special Events
Catering
Chef: Peter Pahk

BAR & GRILL
OPEN DAILY
Breakfast:
6:30am-11:30am
Lunch: 11:30am-5pm
Takeout

Check out the names on the plaques and lockers in this very special room dedicated to the vintners of the Napa Valley. It's where they store the good stuff, and we don't mean golf shoes!

NAPA

WAH SING

1445 Imola Avenue • Napa • (707) 252-0511

CHINESE

OPEN DAILY

LUNCH:
M-F: 11am-3pm
Sa-Su: Noon-3pm
Appetizers: $3-$6
Entrées: $5-$7

DINNER:
4pm-9:30pm
Appetizers: $3-$6
Entrées: $5-$10
Desserts: $3-$4

Corkage: $5
Reservations: Yes

V, MC

Locals' Favorite

Family Friendly

Takeout

Located in Riverpark Shopping Center, *Wah Sing* proudly displays numerous plaques pronouncing them the "Favorite Chinese Restaurant" of local Napans according to an annual poll conducted by the local radio station. Brown paper bags lined up at the cash register are indicative of a brisk takeout business, but this is also a very pleasant spot for in-house dining. Carved teak, painted screens, upholstered chairs, and white tablecloths create a pleasing ambience. The extensive menu features all the usual favorites, and the "daily specials" are definitely worth a try. The chefs put a California spin on many favorite dishes, often substituting seasonal, locally grown vegetables for the usual beans or peas. For example, the asparagus with beef is outstanding: tender, sliced beef with asparagus tips done to perfection in a mildly spicy mandarin sauce. All specials are available for takeout, so ask about them when calling. Several Chinese beers are available. Only a few wines are offered, so BYO is highly recommended.

Have dinner here before a play at Dreamweavers Theatre, at the rear of Riverfront Plaza. There are performances most weekends. Call 255-5483 or visit dreamweaverstheatre.org.

ADVENTURES IN DINING

NAPA

ZINSVALLEY

3253 Browns Valley Road • Napa • (707) 224-0695

AMERICAN

Two wood-burning fireplaces keep this popular spot cozy during the winter months, but when the weather is nice, the best seats in the house are on the back patio, where tables are scattered around a flower filled oasis populated with shade-giving trees or umbrellas. The "Zin" in *Zinsvalley* refers to the unique wine list, featuring over 35 zinfandel wines, many from award-winning zin-only producers. Sixty more selections include some of the best whites and reds from the Napa and Sonoma Valleys, plus a great selection of wines by the glass. Owner Greg Johnson was formerly Executive Sous Chef at *Auberge du Soleil* and *Mustards* before opening *Zinsvalley.* His inspired California cuisine features soups, salads, fresh fish, steak, chicken, and a pizza of the day. The appetizers are wonderful: crispy calamari, artisan cheeses, duck confit and smoked trout are a few favorites The desserts are fabulous. "Greg's Coffee and Donuts," two homemade donuts with a chocolate mocha custard, was featured in *Bon Appetit* last year!

CLOSED SUNDAYS
LUNCH Wed, Th, Fri:
11:30am-2:30pm
Appetizers: $4-$9
Entrées: $9-$16
Desserts: $6-$7

DINNER:
M-Th: 5pm-9pm
Fri-Sa: 5pm-9:30pm
Appetizers: $4-$9
Entrées: $13-$18
Desserts: $6-$7

Pizza
Winning Wine List
Corkage: $15
Reservations: Yes

V, MC
Locals' Favorite
Family Friendly
Special Events
Takeout

Chef: Dylan Rayher

Be sure to try their special "zin tasting" trio, a wonderful way to sample and compare featured wines. Also: A special Bistro Meal for just $25 is featured Monday-Thursday nights.

NAPA

ZUZU

829 Main Street • Napa • (707) 224-8555

MEDITERRANEAN

OPEN DAILY

LUNCH:
11:30am-4pm

DINNER:
M-Th: 4pm-10:30pm
Fri-Sa: 4pm-12am

Prices: $3-$11
Desserts: $5-$6

Continuous Dining
Late Kitchen
Corkage: $10
Reservations: No

V, MC, AE
Locals' Favorite
Catering
Takeout

Chef: Charles Weber

What a fun place to meet friends and enjoy a glass of wine and a bite to eat! Chances are you'll find yourself ordering *many* bites at this downtown Napa tapas bar and calling it dinner. If so, you'll learn first hand why this new "in" spot is so popular. *Zuzu's* is quite small, but the dark, Mediterranean-style décor is decidedly hip. Eat at tables or the bar downstairs, or upstairs in the loft overlooking the action. Reservations aren't taken. Traditional Spanish tapas can be as simple as a dish of olives or as hearty as a small potato tortilla. Chef Charles Weber's creative flair takes this concept to a new level, with dozens of "small plate" options, from anchovies to tapenades, paella to lamb sausage. Unique combinations of flavors result in Serrano ham sauced with a Piquillo Pepper Vinaigrette, or seared tuna with jicama, grapefruit, avocado and papaya. Rely on the energetic and attentive wait staff for recommendations on both the food and wine. The international wine list has been chosen with care and offers many moderately priced bottles.

Order the tapas toppings ($4) of cheese, garlic, peppers, and beans to sprinkle on top for an extra kick. FYI: Nobody serves later than Zuzu on weekends in downtown Napa (12am)!!

ADVENTURES IN DINING

NAPA

GENOVA
1550 Trancas • Napa • (707) 253-8686

ITALIAN DELI • WINE • BEER

Expect sensory overload the moment you walk in the door. The tantalizing aromas immediately get your attention, but it's the number of choices that will really knock your socks off. Choose from six different salamis, five types of turkey, assorted cheeses and a variety of other meats to custom design your own sandwich, or select one of *Genova's* 17 American, 18 Italian or 10 pre-made specialty sandwiches. Selecting a salad isn't easy either with over 27 choices! If you prefer something hot, check out the prepared foods: try a bowl of minestrone soup, some lasagna, or perhaps eggplant Parmesan. *Genova* is one-stop shopping at its best: fantastic desserts, great wine selections, cold beer and soft drinks are all available. Great for takeout, but there are also a few tables inside and outside.

The freezer case is full of boxes of *Genova's* famous ravioli and sauces to take home! Browse the central display area for imported dried pasta, beans and grains in bulk, anchovies, marinated vegetables and freshly baked bread.

OPEN DAILY
M-Sa: 9am-6:30pm
Su: 9am-5pm

Wine • Beer

V, MC, DC

Call ahead and have them make up a platter of your favorite antipasti, add a container of lasagna, a green salad, and cheesecake and you have a party to go!

NAPA

MONTICELLO DELI & CATERING COMPANY
1810 Monticello Road • Napa • (707) 255-3953

DELI • ESPRESSO • WINE BAR • GIFTS

CLOSED SUNDAYS
HOURS:
M-F: 7am-6pm
Sa: 8am-3pm

BREAKFAST:
M-F: 7am-10:30am
Sa: 8am-11am
Prices: $4-$7

LUNCH ALL DAY
Sandwiches: $6

Espresso
Wine Bar
Corkage: None

V, MC, AE, DC

Catering

In a former life, this company was located in Oakville and called *Pometta's*, practically an icon in the Napa Valley for many years. In 2002, the company resurfaced in Napa under a new name, *Monticello Deli & Catering Company*. They also hired the very talented Chef Armando who had been at *The Diner* in Yountville for 14 years. If you are planning a picnic for a large group and don't want to fuss, pick up the phone and place your order, preferably 24 hours ahead. They'll prepare the whole thing, including dessert, for a very reasonable price. *Monticello* is more than a just a takeout mecca, it's also a nice little café with plenty of seating inside and out. A wine bar offering several selections of red and white wines daily adds a very nice touch. Sandwiches, salads, roasted chicken, cookies and wine are all available from 6:30am until closing. Check out their selection of specialty foods and gift items.

Monticello has an Espresso Bar and serves breakfast beginning at 7am weekdays, 8am on weekends.

Delicious box lunches including choice of entrée, salad and dessert can be ordered ahead for only $13.50.

NAPA

NAPA GENERAL STORE & WINE BAR
540 Main Street • Napa • (707) 259-0762

DELI • WINE TASTING • GIFTS • HOUSEWARES

Located on the river in the historic Hatt Building, this brand-new establishment is a delicatessen, specialty market, restaurant, and Wine Bar. Owner/Manager Jill Brandt teamed up with Chef Aram Chakarain, formerly of *Tuscany*, to create downtown Napa's first gourmet market. Not only are they set up nicely for catering, picnic provisioning and pre-ordering, they deliver and hope to become the "personal pantry" for local weekenders. Once a warehouse, the expansive space retains that "industrial" feel, with concrete floors and exposed brick. A large outdoor patio fronts the Napa River, making it a natural for private parties and special events. Breakfast foods include bagels, muffins, scones and espresso. Salads and made-to-order New York-style deli sandwiches are available from 10am-6pm, rotisserie chicken and thin-crust 9" brick oven pizza from 11am-6pm. Daniel Reese runs the attractive and spacious Wine Bar, where five reds and five whites from around the world in a variety of price ranges can be tasted daily. Tasting a flight of five wines is $5.

OPEN DAILY

HOURS: 9am-7pm

Sandwiches: $5-$8
Pizza: $8-$10

Espresso

Wine Bar

V, MC

Special Events

Catering

Chef:
Aram Chakarain

The Gondola Servizio Napa office is located in the same building. Create your own feast and glide down the Napa River in an authentic Venetian Gondola! Call (707) 257-8495.

NAPA

BUTTER CREAM BAKERY & CAFÉ
2297 Jefferson Street • Napa • (707) 255-6700

BAKERY • RESTAURANT

OPEN DAILY
BAKERY HOURS:
5:30am-7pm
Su: 5:30am-2pm

BREAKFAST
Served until 4pm
Prices: $4-$7

LUNCH:
10:30am-4pm
Prices: $5-$8

Hamburgers

Continuous Dining

Reservations: No

V, MC

Locals' Favorite

Family Friendly

Anyone with fond memories of an old-fashioned, neighborhood bakery should not miss the pink and white striped, aptly named *Butter Cream*. This is the kind of place where the women behind the counter still wear aprons and call you "Honey." Sad to say the pink Naugahyde booths were replaced with tables during the recent remodeling but the "soda shop" style counter and pink stools survived. Don't even think of asking for low-fat here! Rich coffee cakes, butter and pecan horns, bear claws, Danish with every imaginable filling, scones, fritters and cinnamon rolls fly out the door each morning, replaced by cookies, brownies, and cakes in the afternoon. And that's just for starters, since *Butter Cream* also serves breakfast and lunch. Breakfasts are big and basic. The affinity for butter carries over to anything cooked on a griddle. Lunchtime soups and sandwiches are quite tasty; there are even a few that aren't grilled!

Butter Cream makes a dynamite Wine Cake (it's the size of a small bundt cake). It's made with red wine and is absolutely delicious. They also make wedding cakes.

ADVENTURES IN DINING

SWEET FINALE PATISSERIE
1146 Main Street • Napa • (707) 224-2444

BAKERY • CAFÉ

Sweet Finale has long been considered one of BEST bakeries in Napa Valley, or anywhere else for that matter. Up until recently, your best bet for one of their amazing creations was at one of the specialty markets, like *Sunshine Foods* in St. Helena (who will continue to carry them). Now that they have opened their own little patisserie on Main Street in downtown Napa, you can go right to the source for the ultimate in caloric indulgence. These culinary masterpieces actually lend themselves to architectural drawings exposing layer upon layer of wafers, mousses, chocolates, berries and ganaches (no kidding–they were posted in the windows prior to the grand opening)! With dessert names like Razmatazz, Phantom of the Opera, Angel and the Devil, and Chai-Chai-Chai, who can resist?

Sweet Finale offers espresso drinks, teas, and breakfast pastries, plus a few "light lunch" items, e.g. quiche. They also plan to stay open until 10pm any night the Napa Valley Opera is active, just a few doors away.

CLOSED MONDAYS

HOURS:
T-Th: 7am-6pm
F-Sa: 7am-2:30pm
       5pm-8pm
Su: 9am-5pm

Espresso

Light Lunch

V, MC

Pastry Chefs:
Joan & Tim
Ketchmark

Sweet Finale specializes in wedding cakes, often decorating them with a Wine Country theme. Marzipan is hand-molded to form the individual grapes in each cluster!

NAPA

SWEETIE PIES
520 Main Street • Napa • (707) 257-7280

BAKERY • ESPRESSO • CAFÉ • SMOOTHIES

OPEN DAILY
M-W: 6:30am-5pm
Th-Sa: 6:30am-6pm
Su: 7am-2pm

BREAKFAST: $3-$5
LUNCH: $4-$6

Espresso

V, MC

Locals' Favorite

Chef: Toni Chiapetta

Located in the historic Hatt Building on the Napa River, this little gem of a bakery supplies many of the top-end specialty markets all over the Valley and is a delightful place for a morning espresso with something fresh from the oven. You'll find a wonderful selection of oversized muffins, scones, Danish, bearclaws, croissants and sticky buns. The homemade granola, fruit and yogurt parfaits, breakfast croissants, and quiches are also delicious. At lunchtime there are always a few specials including a vegetable quiche and pizzetta. Come here anytime for unique and very special desserts: cakes, pies, tarts, cheesecakes, incredible bars and cookies–they are all winners. There are a half a dozen tables inside and a few café tables on the sidewalk in front. Treat the rest of your family or friends and take home a whole coffee cake or quick bread. If you need to order a special occasion "anything," *Sweetie Pies* is the place.

The Hatt Building was a warehouse and mill from the late 1800's to early 1900's. Sweetie Pies contains an original piece of milling equipment–check out the chute and bagging device!

NAPA

CAFFINO • NV ROASTING CO • STARBUCKS

BEST BETS FOR EARLY MORNING ESPRESSO

CAFFINO

This conveniently located drive-thru in the Bel Aire Shopping Center on Trancas has arguably the best espresso drinks in the Valley. They are certainly the most consistent!

NAPA VALLEY COFFEE ROASTING CO

Pleasant coffeehouse located on the corner of First and Main in downtown Napa. This is the sister location to the original Napa Valley Roasting Company in St. Helena.

STARBUCKS

Starbucks seems to be everywhere these days, but they're NOT Upvalley! There are, however, 3 locations in Napa with all of the things we've come to expect. The Soscol location also has a drive-thru!

CAFFINO
3950 Bel Aire Plaza
M-Th: 5am-9pm
Fri-Sa: 5am-10pm
Su: 6am-9pm

NAPA VALLEY
ROASTING CO.
948 Main Street
7am-6pm Daily

STARBUCKS
1340 Trancas
M-Th: 4:30am-9pm
F-Sa: 5am-10pm
Su: 5:30am-9pm

663 Trancas
M-F: 5:30am-9pm
Sa: 6am-9pm
Su: 6:30am-9pm

253 Soscol
M-Th: 4:30am-10pm
F-Sa: 4:30am-11pm
Su: 4:30am-9:30pm

If you're looking for another excellent downtown location, Sweetie Pies Bakery, listed on the preceding page, serves espresso starting at 6:30am.

NAPA

PARSLEY...& BOB • CAFÉ SOCIETY • TRADITIONS

ESPRESSO & MORE

PARSLEY SAGE ROSEMARY & BOB

PARSLEY SAGE
ROSEMARY & BOB
1248 First St., Napa
M-Sa 10am-5:30pm
Closed Sundays

The name alone is reason enough to visit! Specialty food products, sandwiches, fancy oils and vinegars, great gifts and gift baskets, gourmet candy, plus an espresso bar in the back make this shop as unique as its name. And yes, there is a Bob.

CAFÉ SOCIETY

CAFÉ SOCIETY
1000 Main St., Napa
M-Th: 7am-6pm
Fri: 7am-10pm
Sa: 10am-10pm
Su: 10am-6pm

Think French: Croissants, baguettes, French Lemonade, gelato and of course, Café au Lait. Half the store is devoted to "European Antiques and Assessories" which makes browsing mandatory. Even the beautiful hand-woven bistro tables and chairs are for sale! It's just 2 doors from the Napa Valley Opera House.

NAPA VALLEY TRADITIONS

NV TRADITIONS
Main & Pearl, Napa
M-F: 7:30am-5:30pm
Sa: 9am-5:30pm
Su: 10am-4pm

Located at the corner of Main and Pearl, *Traditions* is best described as a really fantastic gift shop that just happens to serve espresso. You'll find lots of unique wine-related gift ideas as well as home accessories, books, cards and dozens of teddy bears.

Another great spot, Sweet Finale Patisserie, is located directly across the street from Traditions, and a few doors down from Cafe Society. Sweet Finale is listed under Napa Bakeries.

NAPA

ANETTE'S CHOCOLATE FACTORY
1321 First Street • Napa • (707) 252-4228

ICE CREAM • CANDY • ESPRESSO • GIFTS

Anette's has the best ice cream in downtown Napa. The "frozen granite slab ice cream cone" is a must: choose from 15 flavors of homemade ice cream and whatever "mix-in" you want. One scoop with one mix-in is $2.95. Metal spatulas are used to blend and chop everything together. *Anette's* is also an amazing candy store–everything (including the ice cream) is made on site! Delectable samples of candies tempt you at every turn. Candied nuts, fudges, truffles, creams, and brittles are absolutely world-class. Do not miss the wonderfully decadent Wine Truffles ($17.95/lb and up). We especially like the dainty size because they're easier to consume when no one is looking. Don't miss Brent's (Anette's brother) Chocolate Wine & Liqueur Sauces in seven flavors: Chocolate Cabernet, Port, Orange Liqueur, Raspberry Liqueur, Amaretto, Butterscotch Scotch, and Dark Chocolate Belgian Liqueur ($8.95 for 5 ounces and $17 for 12.5 ounces). They're great in coffee or drizzled over fruit or your favorite desserts.

OPEN DAILY

HOURS:
M-F: 9:30am-6:30pm
Sa: 10am-6pm
Su: 11:30am-4pm

Café

Candy

V, MC, AE

Owners:
Anette & Brent
Madison

Check out the many gift ideas: fancy hand-painted ice cream scoops and pizza cutters, decorative boxes, tins, and baskets of all shapes and sizes, and Anette's decadent gift baskets.

NAPA

COLD STONE CREAMERY
651 Trancas (Silverado Plaza) • Napa • (707) 251-3707

ICE CREAM • SMOOTHIES

OPEN DAILY
M-Th: 11am-10pm
Sa: 11am-11pm
Su: 1pm-10pm

WINTER HOURS:
Close 9pm weekdays

V, MC, AE, DC

Special Events

Catering

Owner: Tom Bailey &
7 kids!

This is the ultimate in ice cream stores! Grab a seat at one of the small tables inside or out, and enjoy an ice cream masterpiece of your own creation. That's right! Start by choosing from over 25 homemade ice cream and yogurt flavors as the base. Next, add as many "mix-ins" as you like from over 35 selections, such as favorite candy bars, fruit, nuts, and other great stuff. The super premium ice cream and yogurt are made in the store fresh each morning and frozen to the perfect consistency. Once your selections have been made, the ice cream is scooped onto a frozen slab of granite where the "mix-ins" are folded into the ice cream by hand (using a unique Italian spade). Now for even more choices: freshly baked waffle cone or bowl? Dipped or drizzled? How about a few more toppings? Finally the moment of truth arrives and you get to eat this creation, and what a treat it is! Just remember Miss Piggy's invaluable advice: "Never eat more than you can lift."

P.S. The Smoothies are great too!

Talk about the ultimate party: Hire Cold Stone's mobile unit to come out or order a custom designed ice cream cake or pie to pick up at the store.

CHEF'S MARKET
Napa Town Center & First Street

PRODUCE • WINE & FOOD • CRAFTS • MUSIC

As much Street Faire as Farmers Market, the *Chef's Market* is really just a good excuse to head downtown. Sure, there's terrific produce, cut flowers, and Napa and Sonoma specialty food products, but there are also cooking demonstrations, four live entertainment areas, three beer and wine gardens, and lots of dining opportunities. Families come down and make a night of it; there are even planned activities for the kids. Downtown shops stay open later than usual, and many nearby restaurants feature special menus or lighter fare especially for Market Night. The beer and wine gardens offer a variety of microbrews and wines by the glass from local wineries, plus a specially featured "Winery of the Week." Live entertainment usually begins around 6pm.

SEASONAL
LAST FRIDAY
IN MAY THRU
SEPTEMBER
Napa Town Center &
First Street

Fridays: 4pm-9pm

Beer Garden

Wine Tasting

New in 2002: Take a ride on the historic downtown trolley. It makes 14 stops, including Napa Town Center, COPIA, and the Napa Premium Outlet Stores. It's free!!

FARMERS MARKET & ROADSIDE STANDS
West Street between Pearl & First Street

SPECIALTY FOODS • PRODUCE • CAFE

DOWNTOWN NAPA FARMERS MARKET
West Street between Pearl & First Streets

SEASONAL
MAY-OCTOBER
Tues: 7:30am-Noon

Café
Flowers
Produce
Family Friendly
Entertainment

DOWNTOWN FARMERS MARKET The unique downtown location makes this Farmers Market a favorite of local business people who start their day with coffee, conversation and a croissant in the Market Café and Bakery. The Café alone is worth a visit, featuring the very best from nearly every bakery in town. The number of briefcases goes down and the number of baby strollers goes up as the morning wears on. Fresh produce, specialty food products, and fresh-cut flowers are top-notch. Live entertainment and carefully selected arts and crafts vendors complete the picture.

ROADSIDE STANDS
Silverado Trail, north of Trancas

SEASONAL
MAY-JULY

Strawberries

SILVERADO TRAIL STRAWBERRIES A sure sign that summer has arrived is the opening of two strawberry stands on Silverado Trail, less than a mile from Trancas. Nearly surrounded by vineyards, these patches produce the most succulent strawberries imaginable. They're picked early each morning, and only when they are perfectly ripe. People drive from miles around to buy these berries. Pints cost about $1.25. The length of the season varies, beginning in May.

From the Downtown Farmers Market, head one block west to Main Street. Admire the recently restored Opera House, which had its grand reopening in June 2002. Pick up a schedule!

ADVENTURES IN DINING

NAPA

TOP NAPA PICNIC SITES
WHEN AT A WINERY, BUY WINE FROM YOUR HOST

SKYLINE • MONTICELLO • CLOS DU VAL

SKYLINE WILDERNESS PARK is great for hiking and picnicking, where more than a dozen trails of various lengths and degrees of difficulty await. On a clear day, the Rim Rock Trail is a dream (moderate, 3.5 miles round-trip). At the top you'll be rewarded with panoramic views all the way to San Francisco and the Golden Gate Bridge!

SKYLINE HOURS:
Open Daily 8am-5pm
2201 Imola Ave
(Imola & Fourth Ave)
$4 entry fee per car
(707) 252-0481

MONTICELLO VINEYARDS – The Corley family decided to honor wine connoisseur Thomas Jefferson when designing the signature building of their winery, which is a replica of Thomas Jefferson's beloved home. Picnic on the lawns next to Jefferson House while enjoying award-winning Chardonnay and Cabernet wines.

MONTICELLO
Open Daily
10am-4:30pm
4242 Big Ranch Rd
(707) 253-2802
Tasting fee: $7.50
Bottles start at $18

CLOS DU VAL's stellar location affords panoramic views of the famous Stags Leap District. The wide variety of red and white wines produced are highly regarded and reasonably priced. Tasting is complimentary with a tour. Picnic under the oaks and try a game of Pentanque, the French version of Bocce Ball.

CLOS DU VAL
Open Daily
10am-5pm
5330 Silverado Trail
(707) 259-2200

Tasting fee: $5
Bottles start at $18

On Hwy 29 just north of the Hwy 12 East (Fairfield) intersection, there are 2 interesting diversions offering tours: Hakusan Sake Gardens and Seguin Moreau USA Barrel Company.

NAPA

NAPA NITE LIFE

LIVE MUSIC • DJ'S • DANCING

SILVERADO RESORT
1600 Atlas Peak Rd
(707) 257-0200

No cover

SILVERADO COUNTRY CLUB & RESORT features music in the lounge Friday and Saturday nights from 9pm-1am. The band primarily plays jazz and blues, but does take requests. There is a dance floor and no cover charge.

DOWNTOWN JOE'S
902 Main Street
(707) 258-2337
Live Music:
Tu,Th, Su:
8:30pm-2am
Fri-Sa: 9:30pm-2am
$5 cover Fri; $3 Sat

DOWNTOWN JOE'S - This popular brew pub/restaurant is definitely the liveliest spot in town! Open mic on Tuesdays, Blues Jam Session every Thursday, live bands Friday and Saturday, DJ and dancing every Sunday. No cover Tues, Thurs, or Sun; $5 on Friday; $3 on Saturday. Open daily for lunch and dinner, serving until around 1am.

SAKETINI LOUNGE
3900 Bel Aire Plaza
(707) 255-7423
Open Daily 5pm-2am
Music begins 9:30pm

$5 cover Fri & Sat

SAKETINI ASIAN LOUNGE adjoins Saketini Asian Restaurant in Bel Aire Plaza. The Lounge has a DJ spinning tunes most nights, remaining open until around 2am. The place really comes alive on weekends, when it's packed. There's not much in the way of atmosphere or even a place to sit down, but no one cares. It's the music and dance floor that attract the 20-and 30-something crowd. Cover charge on weekends.

The Uptown Theater located on Third Street is currently undergoing renovation and is expected to open in May 2003.

ADVENTURES IN DINING

NAPA

NAPA NITE LIFE

MORE LIVE MUSIC • CONCERTS

UVA TRATTORIA has live jazz every Wednesday and Thursday night from 6:30pm-9:30pm. The band sets up near the Enoteca (food and wine tasting bar), so you have the option of enjoying cocktails and "assaggini" ("little tastes") in the bar or dining in the popular restaurant. (See Napa Restaurants.)

UVA TRATTORIA
1040 Clinton Street
(707) 255-6646

Live Jazz Wed & Th
6:30pm-9:30pm

JARVIS CONSERVATORY OPERA NIGHT The first Saturday of every month is Opera Night at Jarvis Conservatory. Singers and would-be divas from all over the area come to perform in front of an appreciative audience. There's an accompanist, but bring your own music. Babe Pallotta performs on the accordion during intermission! Curtain at 8pm, doors open at 7:30pm.

JARVIS
1711 Main Street
(707) 255-5445
$15 at the door only

Wine & tapas at
intermission.

NAPA VALLEY SYMPHONY season typically runs from October to April, with two performances per month. Each program features a different world-class guest artist. Concerts in 2002-03 are performed in Chardonnay Hall, Napa Expo, 575 Third Street. Concert times are 3pm Sundays, 8pm Tuesdays.

NV SYMPHONY
(707) 226-8742

2002-03 Schedule:
11/10 & 12; 1/12 & 14;
3/2 & 4; 3/29, 30 & 4/1

The Symphony performs a special "Pops" concert at Robert Mondavi Winery as part of the Summer Music Festival. Picnic on the lawn before the concert! Tentative date 6/28/03.

NAPA NITE LIFE

CONCERTS • THEATER • MOVIES

COPIA CONCERTS
500 First Street
(707) 259-1600
Time: 8pm
Tickets: Usually $20

COPIA MONDAY NIGHT CONCERTS can be as different as *"Great American Tunesmiths"* and *"A Cappella Slam,"* but the calibre of performance is usually outstanding. Not only are these concerts entertaining, they're a great value.

NV REP performs at Native Sons of the Golden West Hall
937 Coombs

Box Office:
(800) 557-NVRT

NAPA VALLEY REPERTORY THEATER Napa's first professional theater company was born in 2001. The Napa Rep is a company to watch–they have big dreams with big talent to back it up. If you love theater, this is about as pure and simple as it gets, and great fun too. For upcoming shows visit www.naparep.com.

COPIA FLICKS
500 First Street
(707) 259-1600
Time: 8pm
Tickets: $6

COPIA FRIDAY NIGHT FLICKS always have a monthly theme, e.g. "Honoring Our Heritage" or "In the Garden." The movies are not first-run, most are independent or foreign films, and all have distinguished themselves in some way through awards and/or critical acclaim.

CINE DOME
825 Pearl (at Soscol)
(707) 257-7700

CINE DOME THEATERS is Napa's only movie theater complex.

COPIA, the American Center for Wine Food and the Arts is a beehive of activity: art exhibits, cooking demonstrations, lectures, and wine tastings. Visit www.copia.org for a schedule.

ADVENTURES IN DINING

NAPA

NAPA NITE LIFE

NAPA VALLEY OPERA HOUSE

When the newly restored *Napa Valley Opera House* reopened November 15, 2002, 88 years had passed since it had seen its last public performance. The restoration project took nearly 20 years from the first twinkle in a benefactor's eye to completion, and close to $10 million in donations. Performances currently take place in the 200-seat Café Theatre on the ground floor, where scheduling has been nicely diversified and first rate, including top names like Wesla Whitfield and Kitty Margolis. In mid-2003, the restoration of the 500-seat Main Theater upstairs will be completed, enabling the Opera House to attract world-class musical theater, dance and opera productions.

The complete schedule of upcoming performances can be found on their website, napavalleyoperahouse.org or call (707) 226-7372.

NAPA VALLEY OPERA HOUSE

1030 Main Street
(707) 226-7372

The Café Theatre is also available for special events. There are gorgeous wood bars lining two sides of the room and fully equipped catering facilities in back.

NAPA

NAPA NITE LIFE

THEATER • GONDOLA RIDE • POETRY & MUSIC

DREAMWEAVERS
1637 Imola Avenue
(707) 255-5483

Located at the back
of River Park Plaza

Tickets are $15

DREAMWEAVERS THEATER makes theater accessible to as many people as possible, encouraging hands-on participation in some aspect of a play's production, or simply as a member of the audience. This is not professional theater, but it is fun, with productions every other month, most weekends. Call or check www.dreamweaverstheater.org for a schedule.

GONDOLA SERVIZIO
500 Main Street
(866) 737-8494
By Appt Only
$125 / hour for 2
Dock located at Main
and Third Streets

GONDOLA SERVIZIO is *certainly* the most romantic nite life activity Napa has to offer. Imagine gliding down a moonlit Napa River in an authentic Venetian gondola, with gondolier Angelino Sandri singing Italian love songs! This is an experience you won't soon forget.

CAFÉ SOCIETY

1000 Main Street
(707) 256-3232

Poetry readings free
Live Music: $12-$14
at the door.

CAFÉ SOCIETY – This cute French café serves café au lait, baguettes, croissants and gelato and is the meeting place for the Napa Chapter of Alliance Française. They also host poetry readings on the first Tuesday of each month, from 7:30pm-9pm. On the last Thursday of each month, there's live music from 7pm-9pm.

If gliding down the Napa River sounds like fun (and it is), rent a kayak for a few hours from Napa River Adventures. Call Kevin at (707) 224-9080.

Yountville

Bouchon

Yountville

Founded in the mid 1800's by George C. Yount, this small town has it all...except for a "downtown"! There are four shopping areas, over a dozen restaurants, a golf course, bocce ball courts, parks, hot air balloons, wineries, the Napa Valley Museum, and plenty of elegant places to spend the night.

Yountville has played a very important role in the development of the Napa Valley as a world-class wine producing area. It began as part of a land grant from General Vallejo to George C. Yount of nearly 12,000 acres located in the middle of Napa Valley. Since only Mexicans and Indians could be landowners at that time, Vallejo baptized Yount as Jorge de Concepcion Yount and made him a Mexican citizen. Yount began designing and building the town he named Sebastopol. He also planted the first grapevines in Napa Valley from cuttings given to him from Vallejo. The town was renamed Yountville in his honor in 1867, two years after his death. In 1870 Gottlieb Groezinger, another immigrant, moved into the area from San Francisco and built a large brick winery. This building now houses the shopping complex called Vintage 1870. You can find more information about this fascinating time in history in the beautiful Napa Valley Museum.

ADVENTURES IN DINING

Yountville has a population of just over 2,300 and covers just 1.5 square miles. This includes the section on the west side of Hwy 29 where the Veterans Home, the Napa Valley Museum and Domaine Chandon are located. On the east side, you an easily walk from one end to the other in less that 20 minutes. However, with over 40 shops, galleries, and restaurants located along the way, it will probably take you much longer.

With its own golf course, bocce ball courts, and some of the best roads for bicycling in Napa Valley, Yountville is also a haven for outdoor adventures. For a truly unforgettable experience, be sure to get up early so you can see the hot air balloons get ready to launch from the parking lots at Domaine Chandon and Vintage 1870. It is an awesome sight! You might even decide to go for a ride yourself!

Food is a very important part of the Yountville scene. It is the home of the world-famous *French Laundry* as well as several other small restaurants routinely ranked among the best in the Bay Area.

Throughout the year, Yountville hosts numerous festivals and celebrations. A few favorites include Taste of Yountville Days, the Italian Festival and the Festival of Lights. This popular holiday festival begins the Friday after Thanksgiving with a huge Street Faire, culminating in the town lighting, when tens of thousands of tiny lights are illuminated. No matter what time of year you visit, you will be amazed to discover how much this little town has to offer.

YOUNTVILLE

YOUNTVILLE

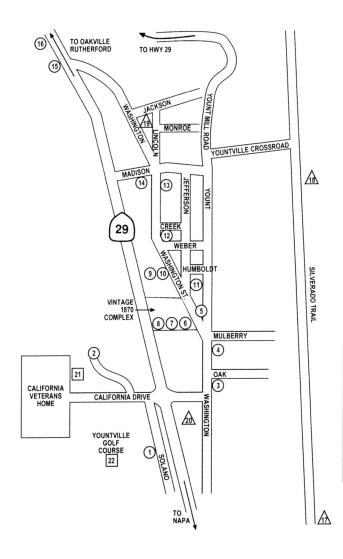

Notes

ADVENTURES IN DINING

BISTRO JEANTY

6510 Washington Street • Yountville • (707) 944-0103

FRENCH

When Chef Philippe Jeanty left *Domaine Chandon* to open his own restaurant, great things were expected. Jeanty succeeded with flying colors, creating a wonderfully unique brasserie that practically screams French Countryside. Unlike its more cosmopolitan neighbor *Bouchon*, *Bistro Jeanty* has a rustic feel, from the stuccoed facade, striped awnings and geranium-filled window boxes to the wood plank floors and decorative French posters. It is an intimate place, with a small dining area as you enter, and a larger one in back. A bar and patio area accommodate those waiting. The single page menu is chock full of famous "Country French" dishes that enjoy fresh and unique presentations à la Jeanty. Wonderful pâtés, escargots, or the tomato soup en croute go perfectly with the Coq au Vin, Cassoulet, or Jeanty's version of Daube de Boeuf (beef stew). Dessert is a calorie splurge, but worth it. *Bistro Jeanty* is an amazing value for food of this caliber.

OPEN DAILY

LUNCH / DINNER:
11:30am-10:30pm

Appetizers: $7-$11
Entrées: $14-$23
Desserts: $5-$7

Continuous Dining
Late Kitchen

Wine Bar
Winning Wine List
Corkage: $15
Reservations: Yes

V, MC, AE
Locals' Favorite
Bay Area Top 100

Chef:
Philippe Jeanty

Last-minute reservations are tough, but "drop-ins" are welcome at the "first come, first served" community table in the front dining room.

YOUNTVILLE

BOUCHON

6534 Washington Street • Yountville • (707) 944-8037

FRENCH

OPEN DAILY
LUNCH:
11:30am-2:30pm
DINNER:
5:30pm-10:45pm

Appetizers: $3-$6
Entrées: $14-$22
Desserts: $3-$7

LATE MENU:
10:45pm-12:30am

OYSTER BAR

Late Kitchen
Winning Wine List
Corkage: $15
Reservations: Yes

V, MC, AE
Locals' Favorite
Bay Area Top 100

Chef:
Jeffrey Cerciello

Bouchon means "cork" in French, but also describes a type of brasserie that has been popular in France for centuries. The striking red façade, café tables and potted shrubs immediately conjure up images of gay Paris. Burgundy velvet banquettes, antique light fixtures, mosaic floors, palm trees and a wall mural by French artist Paulin Paris complete the fantasy. A fabulous selection of raw seafood is artfully arranged atop the handcrafted zinc bar, along with three types of caviar. Chalkboards display the daily specials, and brown paper napkin rings double as the menu. This is Classic French cuisine at its best. Standard offerings include French Onion Soup, foie gras ($35 for 5 ounces), and chocolate mousse. The pommes frites spilling out of a paper cone stuck on top of an old-fashioned chrome holder are outstanding. *Bouchon's* late hours make it a popular gathering spot for local luminaries in the restaurant industry. A special late-night menu is served from 10:45pm-12:30am daily. By the way, this is Thomas Keller's "other" restaurant!

Bouchon stays open far later than any other restaurant in the Valley (12:30am daily). Great for lunch or dinner, but also ideal for that late snack, dessert, or nightcap.

BRIX

7377 St. Helena Hwy • Yountville • (707) 944-2749

FUSION

Asian influences in the sophisticated décor are mirrored by the unique culinary "fusion" that distinguishes *Brix* from other fine restaurants. Though located just north of Yountville on busy Hwy 29, all views from the restaurant are trained on the vineyards and mountains to the west. Be sure to request window seating or better yet, ask to sit outside on the lovely patio and enjoy one of the best views in the Valley. From a culinary perspective, nobody has a better, or more varied, seafood selection than Brix. Sample your favorites at their sumptuous Sunday Brunch Buffet along with omelets, crepes, French Toast, and much more for just $18.95 ($8.95 for children). Don't miss the fabulous wine and gift shop which has some of the best prices around for hard-to-find small production California wines, many of which find their way to the restaurant's 450+ bottle wine list. For special events and celebrations for groups of 30 to 60 people, consider renting one of two private rooms, each with incredible vineyard views.

OPEN DAILY
LUNCH:
11am-3pm
Appetizers: $7-$13
Entrées: $9-$21
Desserts: $4-$7
DINNER:
5pm-9:30pm
Appetizers: $8-$17
Entrées: $17-$29
Desserts: $4-$7

Hamburgers (lunch)
Sunday Brunch:
10am-2pm

Winning Wine List
Corkage: $15
Reservations: Yes

V, MC, AE, DC
Locals' Favorite
Romantic Spot
Special Events
Chef: Michael Patton

Brix provides complimentary round-trip limo service Wednesday through Saturday for diners coming from Yountville, to as far north as the Rutherford Crossroad.

ADVENTURES IN DINING

YOUNTVILLE

COMPADRES MEXICAN BAR & GRILL
6539 Washington Street • Yountville • (707) 944-2406

MEXICAN

OPEN DAILY

BREAKFAST:
Sa-Su: 8am-11am
Prices: $8-$11

LUNCH / DINNER:
Su-Th: 11am-9:30pm
F-Sa: 11am-10:30pm
Appetizers: $3-$10
Entrées: $7-$19
Desserts: $5-$8

Continuous Dining
Late Kitchen (F-Sa)
Corkage: None
Reservations: Yes

V, MC, AE, DC
Family Friendly
Special Events
Catering
Takeout

Compadres' attractive southwestern décor, friendly service, extensive menu, and killer margaritas all contribute to the staying power of this popular Mexican restaurant. The style may be too "Americanized" for some, but the menu is diverse enough to please most palates. Two of our favorite dishes are the Carnitas and the Avocado Relleno (both are $14.50). Management welcomes and can nicely accommodate small birthday parties and special events in the main dining room without disturbing other diners, and also offers the private Sun Room (great view) for groups of 15 to 25 at no extra charge. The large patio in the back has vineyard and mountain views, heaters and Mexican Chimneys for those chilly nights. Specify your seating preference when making a reservation. Fortunately there is a good size bar and front porch, because you can expect a wait even with a reservation on the weekend. Breakfast is served Saturday and Sunday mornings only.

Tequila lovers take note: Compadres serves over 50 kinds of tequila! From June through September, enjoy live music on the lawn from 3pm-6pm.

ADVENTURES IN DINING

CUCINA À LA CARTE

6525 Washington Street • Yountville • (707) 944-1600

ITALIAN

New to the Valley in summer of 2002, *Cucina* is located in the rear building of the Vintage 1870 complex. Chef Stefan Richter trained in Europe, recently trading his position as executive sous chef at the Bellagio Hotel in Las Vegas for his own place in the Napa Valley. Here he gets to bake his own bread, make his own pasta, cure the salmon and smoke the trout. The freshness of the ingredients cannot be beat! The menu is truly a mix of French, Italian, and American with breakfast items such as "the quiet frenchman" – a croissant stuffed with scrambled eggs, prosciutto and fontina. Luncheon sandwiches, served with choice of potato salad, pasta salad or french fries, could be as sophisticated as a baguette with house smoked chicken, caramelized onions and lemon tarragon mayo or as simple as tomato, mozzarella and basil with a balsamic vinaigrette. Desserts are mostly gelato or sorbets and well worth the calories. *Cucina* has a nice wine list as well as a full bar. An Espresso Bar opens at 5:30am – by far the earliest spot in town.

OPEN DAILY
BREAKFAST:
5:30am-11am
Prices: $5-$8
LUNCH / DINNER:
11am-9pm
Sandwiches: $7-$10
Entrées: $10-$18
Desserts: $8

Deli
Pizza
Espresso Bar
Opens 5:30am

Continuous Dining
Corkage: $15
Reservations: No

V, MC, AE
Special Events
Catering
Takeout

Chef: Stefan Richter

Special $9 take-out dinners are featured each night. Think large portions of roast leg of lamb, potato au gratin, and seasonal vegetables, for example. A bargain!

YOUNTVILLE

DOMAINE CHANDON
One California Drive • Yountville • (707) 944-2892

FRENCH

CLOSED TUESDAYS
LUNCH:
11:30am-2pm
Appetizers: $9-$45
Entrées: $17-$30
Desserts: $8-$10

DINNER: 6pm-9pm
Appetizers: $9-$45
Entrées: $24-$33
Desserts: $8-$12

Tasting Menu:
$100 with wine
$65 without wine

Winning Wine List
Corkage: $20
Reservations: Yes

V, MC, AE
Romantic Spot
Special Events
Chef: Eric Torralba

This venerable restaurant will soon be celebrating its 25th anniversary. Esteemed chefs have come and gone, but the quality of the food and the overall dining experience have remained stellar. Signature dishes created by former chef Philippe Jeanty (now of *Bistro Jeanty*) are popular anchors of the menu, but new Executive Chef Eric Torralba adds his own flair to the mix. Not only is the romantic décor coolly elegant, with soaring glass windows overlooking gardens and the surrounding hills, but so are the patrons. You're encouraged to dress up; in the evening jackets for gentlemen are recommended. With sparkling wine the specialty of the house, what more could you ask for? If a more casual experience is desired, go for lunch when recommended dress is "smart casual." The shaded outdoor terrace surrounded by lush gardens is perfect for a summer luncheon. The extensive wine list is exclusively California still and sparkling wines. *Domaine Chandon* brandies are also featured.

Domaine Chandon has many special events, including summer concerts, a Bastille Day Celebration in July, and a film festival in August. Check www.chandon.com for more information.

YOUNTVILLE

FRENCH LAUNDRY
6640 Washington Street • Yountville • (707) 944-2380

FRENCH

Your napkin appears with the signature clothes pin and logo of this outstanding restaurant, referring to the historical use of this 1890's building as a French steam laundry. Surrounded by beautiful gardens, this lovely stone house is an elegant testimony to the sophisticated meals served here. Chef Thomas Keller, named as the best in the country by the James Beard Foundation, has garnered award after award since opening in 1994. The presentation is worth an award all by itself, but it is the delightful and delicious surprise of flavors you find in each bite that really deserves the praise, making eating here a true gastronomic adventure. Be sure to ask the sommelier for pairing suggestions as the daunting wine list is over 50 pages! The taste sensations are so unique, consider choosing half bottles. Reservations are taken exactly two months ahead of the reservation date, so if you hope to be among the chosen few, you MUST plan ahead and make The Call. If that doesn't work, try dropping by at lunchtime—there may be a cancellation or a no-show.

OPEN DAILY
LUNCH:
F-Sa: 11am-1pm
DINNER:
5:30pm-9:30pm

Prix Fixe: $105
Vegetarian: $80

Chef's Tasting Menu:
$120

Wine Bar
Winning Wine List
Corkage: $50
Reservations: Yes

V, MC, AE, DC
Romantic Spot
Bay Area Top 100
Special Events

Chef: Thomas Keller

Someone in your group simply must order the coffee and donut for dessert. Eat your heart out, Crispy Creme! A retail bakery (with ice cream!) will be opening soon.

GORDON'S CAFÉ & WINE BAR
6770 Washington Street • Yountville • (707) 944-8246

CALIFORNIA

CLOSED MONDAYS
BREAKFAST:
Tu-F: 7:30am-11am
Sa-Su: 7:30am-Noon
Prices: $3-$6
LUNCH: 11am-3pm
Prices: $4-$11
DINNER FRI ONLY:
6pm-8:30pm
Prix Fixe: $45

Espresso
Continuous Dining
Wine Bar
Corkage: $15
Reservations:
Friday Dinner Only

V, MC, AE, DC
Locals' Favorite
Family Friendly
Special Events
Catering
Takeout
Chef/Owner:
Sally Gordon

Sally Gordon's neighborhood hang-out for "good food, good company and good times" is a local favorite. Blackboards above the "Order Here" sign announce the daily specials prepared by a team of talented young chefs. Breakfast includes freshly baked treats warm from the oven as well as several egg dishes. Luncheon items include hot and cold sandwiches, soups and prepared salads ideal for picnics. One of the Valley's best-kept secrets is Sally's Friday Night Dinner (3-course prix fixe at $45). Checkered tablecloths, candles and flowers transform *Gordon's* into an utterly charming and romantic café complete with table service. Sally is usually there on Fridays, making sure everyone has a good time. You'll feel like an old friend by the time you've finished dessert. There's a nice wine list, reasonably priced, including 6-8 choices by the glass. Play your cards right and you may get one of the world's best hugs from Sally when you leave! Espresso drinks, takeout and tasting at the Wine Bar are available until closing (5pm) every day (closed Mondays).

Buy one of the terrific wines lining the wall at retail prices and enjoy it with lunch or Friday dinner, with no corkage fee.

HURLEY'S RESTAURANT & BAR
6518 Washington Street • Yountville • (707) 944-2345

CALIFORNIA

Popular local chef Bob Hurley opened his much anticipated new restaurant, *Hurley's*, in November 2002. You'd never believe this place used to be *Livefire*, given the massive remodeling job. Great attention has been paid to every detail, from the wall sconces to the WC, with great results. Light-colored walls show off extensive use of polished mahogany, including a sleek, curved bar. French doors separating a brand new terrace from the bar can be opened up completely, while stone floors and a fireplace add a nice "country" feel. Bob Hurley fans know that no one does California Cuisine better: Fresh fish, steak, rabbit, game hen or pork loin served with side dishes like sautéed spinach, wild mushroom bread pudding, sweet potato flan or potato leek pie are always outstanding. The house specialty, Herb Crusted Blue Nose Sea Bass, is delicious. The all-California wine list (110+) focuses on Napa and Yountville appellations.

The bar serves a separate menu (appetizers, lighter fare) until 12:00am daily.

OPEN DAILY
LUNCH:
11:30am-3:30pm
Appetizers: $6-$12
Entrées: $12-$17
Desserts: $6-$7

DINNER:
Su-Th: 5pm-10pm
F-Sa: 5pm-10:30pm
Appetizers: $6-$9
Entrées: $15-$24
Desserts: $6-$7

BAR MENU:
5:30pm-12:00am

Winning Wine List
Corkage: $10
Reservations: Yes
Late Kitchen

V, MC, AE
Special Events

Chef: Bob Hurley

Bob Hurley was Executive Chef at the Napa Valley Grille in Yountville for many years. It's great to have him back!

LAKESIDE GRILL
7901 Solano Avenue • Yountville • (707) 944-2426

AMERICAN

OPEN DAILY
BREAKFAST:
Sa-Su: 8am-11am
Prices: $5-$8

LUNCH / DINNER:
M-F: 11am-7pm
Sa-Su: 11am-8pm
Prices: $5-$15

Hamburgers
Sunday Brunch
Continuous Dining
Corkage: $7
Reservations: Yes

V, MC, AE
Family Friendly
Special Events
Catering
Takeout

Located in the clubhouse of the Vintner's Golf Course in Yountville, the *Grill* is open seven days a week for lunch and dinner plus breakfast on the weekends. The *Grill* and Pro Shop cohabit a large room with a pleasant southwestern flair, featuring rustic natural wood tables and chairs, a stone fireplace and exposed wood beams. The best seats in the house are outside on the terrace overlooking the golf course and Vintner's Lake, though "lake" is a bit of a stretch. Beautifully landscaped with native California plants and grasses, this man-made pond is a magnet for a variety of songbirds and waterfowl. The food is not fancy: egg dishes, fluffy buttermilk pancakes (outstanding), and French toast for breakfast; sandwiches, salads and burgers for lunch or early dinner. When they're busy, service can be terribly slow, so it's not a good choice if you're in a hurry. On weekends, call ahead to confirm they're open, since the place is often rented out for private events. Happy Hour from 3pm to 6pm, Monday through Friday, features $2 beers and $3 cocktails.

The Vintner's Golf Course and driving range are open to the public. Call 944-1992 for tee times.

ADVENTURES IN DINING

MUSTARDS GRILL

7399 St. Helena Hwy • Yountville • (707) 944-2424

CALIFORNIA

There is something for everyone on the menu here, and there has been for 30 years! Award-winning chef Cindy Pawlcyn opened *Mustards* in 1983, and it has been a favorite hangout ever since for locals as well as millions of visitors. The lively atmosphere and the delicious aromas coming from wood-burning ovens, smokers, and grills are a heady combination! *Mustards* is famous for Pawlcyn's unique "wood-infused" culinary style, and nobody does it better. The doublecut Mongolian pork chop is probably the most popular item on the menu, with the baby back ribs a close second. Fresh fish, duck, lamb, and rabbit are all treated with culinary skill and pair beautifully with the wide assortment of tempting appetizers, soups and salads. Much of the fresh produce comes from the restaurant's own garden at the side of the building. The wine list is carefully chosen and extensive. Desserts are delicious and make perfect endings to a great meal. Be sure to call for a reservation, since this is still a very popular spot both for lunch and dinner.

OPEN DAILY

LUNCH / DINNER:
M-F: 11:30am-9pm
Sa-Su: 11am-10pm

Appetizers: $6-$12
Entrées: $16-$29
Desserts: $5-$7

Hamburgers
Continuous Dining

Winning Wine List
Corkage: $12
Reservations: Yes

V, MC, AE

Chef: Cindy Pawlcyn

YOUNTVILLE

Cindy Pawlcyn's and Brigid Callinan's cookbook, "Mustards Grill Napa Valley Cooking," won the prestigious James Beard Award for Best Americana Cookbook!

NAPA VALLEY GRILLE

Hwy 29 & Madison • Yountville • (707) 944-8686

CALIFORNIA

OPEN DAILY
LUNCH:
11:30am-3pm
Prices: $7-$12
MID-MENU:
3pm-5pm
DINNER:
Su-Th: 5pm-9pm
F-Sa: 5pm-10pm
Appetizers: $6-$12
Entrées: $15-$25
Desserts: $5-$7
SUNDAY BRUNCH
11am-2:30pm
Prices: $9-$14
Continuous Dining
Winning Wine List
Corkage: $15
Reservations: Yes

V, MC, AE
Locals' Favorite
Special Events
Catering
Takeout
Chef: Jude Willmouth

Located at the back of the Washington Square complex, this popular restaurant is known for its oak-fired grill creations. New chef Jude Willmouth was formerly with *Piatti Restaurant* in Sonoma. The menu features daily specials from the grill as well as roasted meats, fish, chicken and vegetarian selections. The full bar features an award-winning wine list with over 800 selections including a complete vertical of Opus One. Dine on the patio with vineyard views or enjoy the nicely appointed interior with its exhibition kitchen. The restaurant is located at the intersection of Hwy 29 and Madison so patio diners can expect a fair amount of road noise. A "Mid-Menu" served from 3pm-5pm offers limited selections from lunch and dinner menus. Attractive private rooms are available for special functions.

The Washington Square Summer Jazz Series features free, live entertainment in the Courtyard, Fridays in August, 6pm-9pm. Ringside seating at The Grille is first come, first served.

YOUNTVILLE

PACIFIC BLUES CAFÉ
6525 Washington Street • Yountville • (707) 944-4455

AMERICAN

When you're tired of fancy food, or your wallet is starting to smoke, this casual café could be just the answer. Espresso drinks and standard breakfast favorites including omelets, pancakes, French toast, and breakfast burritos are served from 8am to11am. Serving continuously throughout the day, salads, sandwiches, burgers, garlic fries, and microbrews rule. The dinner menu expands to include steaks, pork chops and BBQ ribs. The big, juicy burgers are exceptional! Indoor seating is comfortably rustic, and the large outdoor deck facing Vintage 1870 is a pleasant place to people watch, take a break from shopping, or soak up a few rays. A special kids' menu is sure to please the pickiest eater (translation: grilled cheese). Reasonably priced Napa Valley and Sonoma wines are offered by the glass or bottle, and there is a good selection of imported, domestic and microbrew beers. Occasionally there is live music on the weekends.

OPEN DAILY
BREAKFAST:
8am-11am
Prices: $4-$13
LUNCH:
11:30am-9pm
Prices: $6-$12

DINNER: 5pm-9pm
Appetizers: $11-$20
Entrées: $7-$21
Desserts: $6.50

Hamburgers
Microbrews
Espresso
Continuous Dining

Corkage: None
Reservations: No

V, MC, AE
Locals' Favorite
Family Friendly
Takeout

There's nothing like seeing Napa Valley from a hot air balloon! Balloon Flights of Napa Valley is located right next door. They take off around 6:30am from the Vintage 1870 parking lot.

PIATTI RESTAURANT
6480 Washington Street • Yountville • (707) 944-2070

ITALIAN

OPEN DAILY

LUNCH / DINNER:
11:30am-9:30pm

Appetizers: $6-$13
Entrées: $11-$18
Desserts: $6

Pizza
Continuous Dining
Winning Wine List
Corkage: $15
Reservations: Yes

V, MC, AE
Locals' Favorite
Special Events
Catering
Takeout

Chef: Peter Hall

You can always count on *Piatti* for a delicious Italian meal. Locals have been coming here for 15 years, and Chef Peter Hall has been at the helm for the past five. Hand-painted murals on the walls and the heavenly smells of garlic and olive oil wafting from pizzas baking in the wood-burning oven create a warm and comfortable ambience. Lunch or dinner on the patio is just about perfect, with a softly trickling fountain as background music. Trademark dishes such as the ravioli with lemon cream sauce and roasted chicken compete with seasonal daily specials in nearly every category. *Piatti's* famous toasted garlic bread is outstanding and makes a great appetizer. Combine it with a salad and you've got a meal. For dessert, treat yourself to some tiramisu. Every restaurant seems to have a different recipe, and this one is particularly good. Many excellent wines including a few daily specials are available by the glass. The carefully chosen wine list emphasizes Napa and Sonoma Valleys, but also includes many delicious Italian wines.

Piatti gourmet dipping oil and olive tapenade are available for purchase at the restaurant!

YOUNTVILLE

GILLESPIE'S ICE CREAM & CHOCOLATES
6525 Washington Street • Yountville • (707) 944-2113

ICE CREAM • CANDY • NOVELTIES

Located in the Vintage 1870 complex, *Gillespie's* is the only place in Yountville to get a hand-dipped ice cream cone. Happily, the ice cream in question is San Francisco's award-winning Double Rainbow. Nearly three dozen flavors are available, with the usual variations, including shakes, sundaes, and banana splits. If you can't make up your mind, ask for a taste. While you're there, check out the candy. All their fine candies are hand made, but it's the novelty chocolates that are truly unique. You gotta love a guy that's got his own chocolate mold and a sense of humor. This is the place for edible musical instruments, sporting equipment, animals, power tools, motorcycles, trains, plus whimsical multi-piece "themed" sets for firemen, golfers, bowlers, baseball fans, and soccer enthusiasts. The Policeman Set had great looking milk chocolate handcuffs! Gillespie's does a particularly nice job on specialty chocolates for all the major holidays and will priority ship anything within the continental U.S.

OPEN DAILY

HOURS:
M-Th: 10am-5:30pm
F-Sa: 10am-8pm
Su: 10am-7pm

V, MC, AE

YOUNTVILLE

Gillespie's does custom candy creations for all major and minor holidays, perfect for gifts, gags, and stocking stuffers.

YOUNTVILLE FARMERS MARKET
6539 Washington Street • Yountville

PRODUCE • WINE TASTING • COOKING DEMOS

SEASONAL
MAY-OCTOBER
Wed: 4pm-8pm

Wine Tasting

Cooking Demos

Though smaller than the Napa and St. Helena Farmers Markets, the Yountville Farmers Market is further proof that size doesn't matter. Live entertainment, wine tasting, cooking demonstrations and book signings add some sizzle to the usual fresh produce, cut flowers, and specialty foods. Celebrity chefs and local authors, including Chef Thomas Keller, Molly Chappellet (author of *Gardens of the Wine Country*), and photographer Charles O'Rear have all made appearances to chat with shoppers, cook, talk about their latest ventures, and/or sign their latest books. Adding to the fun, each week a different winery hosts a wine tasting. In 2002, the specialty foods were expanded to include cheese, salami, breads, tamales, olive oils, sauces and "homemade" jams and jellies. This market is definitely a "social outing" whether you're shopping for picnic provisons or a gourmet dinner. It also makes a great stop before heading off to dinner at one of Yountville's many fine restaurants.

Yountville is a popular shopping destination. A couple of our personal favorites on Washington are Rasberry's Art Glass Gallery and Mosswood, for home and garden accessories.

TOP YOUNTVILLE PICNIC SPOTS
WHEN AT A WINERY, BUY WINE FROM YOUR HOST

REGUSCI • SINSKEY • TOWN PARKS

REGUSCI WINERY has a Napa address but is closer to Yountville. Constructed from hand-cut volcanic rock in 1897, this historic "ghost winery" stopped production in 1932 due to Prohibition. Restored in 1996 by the Regusci family, it now produces small lots of Chardonnay and a killer Cabernet. Two small picnic areas have spectacular valley views.

REGUSCI WINERY
Open Daily
10am-5pm
5584 Silverado Trail
(707) 254-0403
Appts Requested

Tasting fee: $5
Bottles start at $38

ROBERT SINSKEY VINEYARDS Technically a Napa address, Sinskey is located just south of Yountville Crossroad on Silverado Trail. Picnic tables on the sunny deck have great views across the valley floor to the mountains beyond. Well-known for their award-winning Pinot Noir, Sinskey also produces Merlot, Pinot Blanc, and Chardonnay wines.

SINSKEY VINEYARDS
Open Daily
10am-4:30pm
6320 Silverado Trail
(707) 944-9090

Tasting fee:$10
Bottles start at $30

VETERANS MEMORIAL PARK is tiny but perfectly manicured, and even has a bocce ball court! It's bounded by Hwy 29, California Drive, and Washington Street. GEORGE YOUNT PARK, located at the north end of town, is the primary recreational facility for Yountville residents. Kids will love all the play equipment.

VETERANS PARK
GEO. YOUNT PARK
Open Daily

Visit the Napa Valley Museum located next to the California Veterans Home. Exhibits focus on the local area, including a permanent exhibit: The Making of Wine: the Science of an Art.

YOUNTVILLE NITE LIFE

LATE NITE COCKTAILS

BOUCHON
6534 Washington
(707) 944-8037
Open Daily for lunch
and dinner
Late Menu:
10:45pm-12:30am

HURLEY'S
6518 Washington
(707) 944-2345
Open Daily for lunch
and dinner
Bar Menu served
5:30pm-12:00am

Yountville's nite life centers around the two restaurants that stay open well into the wee morning hours: *Bouchon* and the new kid on the block, *Hurley's Restaurant & Bar*. Fortunately, they both happen to be among the very best restaurants in the Valley. You can be served fabulous food at either place until at least midnight. Both bars remain open until 12:30am.

COMPADRES
6539 Washinton
(707) 944-2406
Open Daily for lunch
and dinner
Su-Th: 11am-10pm
F-Sa: 8am-10:30pm

Compadres Mexican Bar & Grill is the other "sort of" late night spot in town, serving until 10:30pm Friday and Saturday nights, 10pm on weekdays.

DETAILS ON ALL THREE OF THESE RESTAURANTS APPEAR IN THE YOUNTVILLE RESTAURANT SECTION OF THIS GUIDE.

Originally named Sebastopol by founder George Yount, the town was officially renamed Yountville in 1867, two years after his death. Yount is buried in the town cemetery.

Oakville·Rutherford

OAKVILLE
RUTHERFORD

La Toque

Oakville·Rutherford

Located between Yountville and St. Helena are some of some of the most famous wineries, vineyards and appellations in the world. Both of these communities were once part of the 12,000 acres belonging to George Yount. In 1864 Yount's granddaughter, Elizabeth, married Thomas Rutherford, and Yount gave them the 1,040 acres now known as Rutherford as a wedding gift. As the wine industry developed, this area became synonymous with the most famous people and vineyards of the time, such as Gustav Niebaum and Inglenook, George La Tour and Beaulieu Vineyards, and the legendary winemaker Andre Tchelistcheff.

Oakville isn't really a town, it's a zip code! It's also the home of Opus One, Screaming Eagle, Robert Mondavi Winery and the Oakville Grocery, famous for incredible gourmet food and wine. Right across the street from the Oakville Grocery is the Napa Valley Wine Company, where over 60 vintners crush, blend and age their wines. Some of the best boutique wines in the valley are produced right here. Make an appointment at the NVWC Cellar Door for a unique tasting experience, where over 25 wines are available on any given day on a "fee per pour" basis.

On any given weekend during the summer months, there are dozens of activities taking place up and down the valley. One of the most famous annual festivals would certainly be the Robert Mondavi Summer Music Festival, which typically kicks off with the Preservation Hall Jazz Band followed by a spectacular fireworks display the first weekend in July. Picnicking on the lawn prior to the concerts is practically mandatory, and great fun!

Rutherford lies just a few miles north of Oakville on Hwy 29. Stop in and visit the Niebaum-Coppola Estate Winery, where the upstairs gallery houses Francis Ford Coppola's private collection of movie memorabilia, including his Oscars for *The Godfather I & II,* and the Tucker automobile. Directly across the street is historic Beaulieu Vineyards, the oldest continuously operating winery in Napa Valley. Take a tour and you'll learn a lot about the history of the valley, including how Beaulieu managed to stay in business during Prohibition by selling altar wine to the Catholic Church!

Rutherford is also home to La Toque, Rutherford Grill, and across the valley, Auberge du Soleil, one of the top small hotels in the world. The views from the deck at Auberge are spectacular; there's no better place to enjoy a glass of wine while watching the sun set over the Mayacamas mountains.

These two areas may be small in size, but their claim to fame is enormous. Drive too fast and you will miss them both!

OAKVILLE/RUTHERFORD KEY

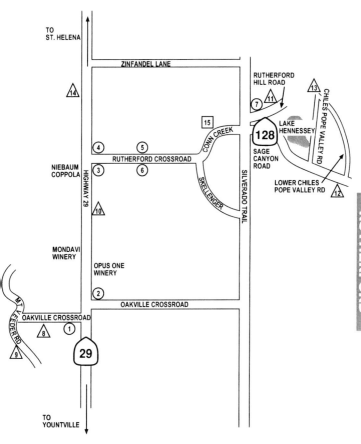

Notes

AUBERGE DU SOLEIL
180 Rutherford Hill Road • Rutherford • (707) 963-1211

CALIFORNIA

Auberge du Soleil has one of the most idylliic settings anywhere in the world. That's right, the WORLD. And that's why you are going to put this on your MUST SEE list. If you're lucky enough to be staying there as a guest, congratulations, the view is included. If not, there are still a couple of ways you can soak up that rarefied atmosphere up on the hill. First, there's the lovely restaurant, open for lunch and dinner, with sweeping views of the valley from any seat inside as well as on the terrace. An elaborate 6-course Prix Fixe menu is $90, and the 4-course Chef's Menu (with choices) is $78. The lunch menu is strictly à la carte. The chef's style can be described as French-inspired California Cuisine.

Dining in the bar is a great option. It's very cozy with nice comfy chairs and its own terrace with the same incredible view. Futhermore, the bar menu is terrific, offering much more than great sandwiches, e.g. calamari with chick peas, red peppers and lemon oil. The Bar serves until 11pm nightly and offers over 20 wines by the glass.

OPEN DAILY
BREAKFAST:
7am-11am
Prices: $16-$19
LUNCH:
11:30am-2:30pm
Appetizers: $10-$18
Entrées: $19-$24
Desserts: $4
DINNER:
6pm-9:30pm
Prix Fixe: $90

Chef's Menu: $78
Winning Wine List
Reservations: Yes
Corkage: $30

BAR HOURS:
11am-11pm
Late Kitchen
V, MC, AE, DC
Romantic Spot
Special Events
Chef:
Richard Reddington

OAKVILLE
RUTHERFORD

Three words to remember: BAR • COCKTAILS • SUNSET
Auberge du Soleil has a view that should NOT be missed!

LA TOQUE
1140 Rutherford Road • Rutherford • (707) 963-9770

FRENCH

CLOSED MON-TUES

DINNER ONLY
2 seatings:
5:30pm and 8:30pm

Prix Fixe: $85
Wine Pairing: $45

Winning Wine List
Corkage: $18
Reservations: Yes

V, MC, AE

Romantic Spot

Bay Area Top 100

Special Events

Chef: Ken Frank

Right from the beginning, Ken Frank's *La Toque* was heralded as one of Napa Valley's finest restaurants. The picturesque stucco building with its red tile roof was once part of the deluxe Rancho Caymus Inn next door, and it still shares that same Old World ambience. A large stone fireplace, polished wood floors, well-spaced tables and an uncluttered decorating scheme set the tone for a comfortable and unhurried dining experience. The knowledgeable staff and measured pace of service encourage the diner to relax and enjoy the elegant presentation of each course. Innovative food combinations are delicious without being contrived and utilize the freshest ingredients from around the world. Vegetarians will be happy to know the vegetarian prix fixe menu receives rave reviews. To further enhance the experience, consider the wine pairing option, where each course is matched with a wine chosen jointly by the chef and sommelier. If you're fond of truffles, be sure to book reservations early for the January "Truffle Menu" Series.

The Napa Valley Grapevine Wreath Company is less than a mile away at 8901 Conn Creek. Their handcrafted wreaths, animals, baskets, and furniture are heirloom quality.

RUTHERFORD GRILL
1180 Rutherford Road • Rutherford • (707) 963-1792

AMERICAN

It's no wonder this reasonably priced restaurant has been a hit with visitors and locals alike since it opened. Located next to Beaulieu Vineyards in Rutherford, it's an easy stop for wine tasters making their way up or down valley. Locals love its comfortable, neighborhood feel that fits the cuisine perfectly: tasty, uncomplicated, American comfort food. Fabulous burgers, steaks, mashed potatoes, BBQ ribs, rotisserie chicken and cornbread are staples. Fans of *Houston's* Restaurant may experience deja vu and recognize many of the signature dishes. You're *not* crazy, *Houston's* owns the place. An enormous dark wood bar dominates the dining room where seating options include comfy leather booths and tables. Weather permitting, patio seating is a pleasant option, with an outdoor fireplace pressed into action during the winter months. No reservations are accepted, so the wait can be quite long. You'll get a pager that flashes when your table is ready. As busy as *Rutherford Grill* is, the service never falters; the servers are knowlegable, friendly, and efficient.

OPEN DAILY

LUNCH / DINNER
Su-Th:
11:30am-9:30pm
F-Sa:
11:30am-10:30pm

Appetizers: $2-$9
Entrées: $9-$26
Desserts: $4-$6

Hamburgers
Continuous Dining
Late Kitchen (F-Sa)
Corkage: None
Reservations: No

V, MC, AE
Locals' Favorite
Family Friendly
Takeout

OAKVILLE
RUTHERFORD

If you want to reduce your wait time, call ahead. They'll be happy to put your name on the list. Beware: your whole party MUST be present before they'll seat you.

NEST CAFÉ & TAKEOUT
7787 St. Helena Hwy • Oakville • (707) 944-0206

DELI • CAFÉ

CLOSED SUNDAYS
HOURS: 7am-6pm

BREAKFAST:
7am until it's gone!
Prices: $3.25-$4

LUNCH ANYTIME!
Sandwiches: $5-$7

DINNERS TO GO

V, MC
Catering

Chefs / Owners:
Kate & Mardi Schma

Everyone who has sorely missed the old *Pometta's Deli* on Oakville Grade will be delighted to learn that in November 2002, a new deli called *Nest* moved in. The new owners are mother-daughter team, Mardi & Kate Schma (pronounced Schmay), originally from Carmel, with a stint in Dallas, Texas, where mom was the chef at a 4-star restaurant, prior to retiring. Kate managed to coax Mom out of retirement and here they are. They've got big plans for this little deli!

Breakfast is served from 7am until they run out, followed by freshly made salads, soups, and sandwiches at lunchtime (remember *Pometta's* wonderful Muffeletta sandwich? It's back, with a Schma spin). Everything, including smoked chicken and brisket and yummy desserts are made on site daily. Try the Texas brisket with BBQ sauce, onion and coleslaw on a French roll, or grilled vegetables with basil pesto and chevre on foccacia. A dinner menu for takeout only features daily specials (like lamb shank or roasted chicken), with your choice of side dishes.

There is plenty of seating inside and on the patio. Be sure to try one of the unusual soft drinks–the names are a riot!

OAKVILLE GROCERY
7856 St Helena Hwy • Oakville • (707) 944-8802

DELI • ESPRESSO • GOURMET FOODS • WINES

No article about Napa Valley is complete without mentioning the venerable *Oakville Grocery*. "Blink and you'll miss it" is not an exaggeration, since the tiny town of Oakville centers around a single crossroad. The old-fashioned building with Coca-Cola emblazoned on the side belongs in a Norman Rockwell painting, were it not located just yards from the ultra-modern Opus One Winery. It may be country on the outside, but it's a cosmopolitan treasure trove of gourmet *everything* inside– a picnicker's paradise with dozens of domestic and imported cheeses, pâtés, vinegars, oils, sauces, chutneys, jams, breads, desserts, and prepared foods. Groups of 8 or more do well pre-ordering the platters that Oakville is famous for. Ask to have a menu faxed. Napa Valley wines in all price ranges are available, including a large selection of half bottles. *Oakville Grocery's* own Chardonnay and Cabernet ($15-$17) produced by Joseph Phelps are bargains. The espresso bar opens at 7am (M-F), 8am (Sa-Su), serving drinks and bakery goods only.

OPEN DAILY

HOURS: 9am-6pm

ESPRESSO BAR
M-F: Open 7am
Sa-Su: Opens 8am

V, MC, AE, DC

Catering

OAKVILLE RUTHERFORD

Delicious box lunches can be pre-ordered 24 hours in advance for $14. Includes your choice of a sandwich, chicken breast or vegetarian entrée, salad, and dessert.

LA LUNA MARKET
1153 Rutherford Road • Rutherford • (707) 963-3211

MEXICAN MARKET • DELI • MEAT COUNTER

OPEN DAILY

MARKET HOURS
Tu-Su: 8am-7pm
Mon: 8am-6pm

KITCHEN HOURS
Tu-Su: 9am-6:30pm
Mon: 9am-5:30pm

Prices: $4-$6

Beer

V, MC

This is THE place to go if you are looking for authentic chorizo, Mexican spices, cheese, and imported hot sauce that can make a fire-breathing dragon weep. Just wandering around this little market is an education. There are things here you won't see anywhere else.

The best part of *La Luna* is the Deli in the back, next to the fresh meats. The menu is posted over the counter (with English translations). Incredible, football-size "super burritos" are filled with your choice of carnitas, al pastor, carne asada or chicken, plus beans, rice, sour cream and avocado. It's really a 3-course meal rolled inside an enchilada, weighing in at close to a pound! Think of it as a dual-purpose burrito: first use it a free weight, then eat it. Needless to say, one super burrito easily feeds 2 people. The super-sized tacos and quesadillas are equally good, one of either would satisfy most appetites.

La Luna is takeout only. They also have an excellent selection of chilled Mexican beer.

If you enjoy cooking, be sure to check out the ridiculously inexpensive packaged spices and herbs. They're a far cry from the bottled stuff we're used to!

ST. HELENA OLIVE OIL COMPANY
8576 St. Helena Hwy • Rutherford • (707) 967-1003

OLIVE OIL • VINEGARS • MUSTARDS • POTTERY

Specialty Market does not accurately describe the *St. Helena Olive Oil Company*. It is really a combination production facility and tasting room for some of the finest, locally made olive oils and vinegars you can find. The retail room is filled with "tasting stations" featuring their many products. Just beyond the tasting room, visitors can see the actual barrels containing red wine vinegars and aging balsamic vinegars, stainless steel vats for the berry vinegars, and in the rear, enormous vats of virgin and extra virgin olive oils. The company's product line goes beyond its many types of olive oil to even more varieties of vinegars. Champagne, Cabernet, and five varieties of berry balsamic vinegars are available. Berry infusions include cherry, strawberry, cranberry, and blueberry. The rest of the retail room is devoted to a wonderfully eclectic assortment of pottery, baskets, linens, chutneys, mustards, cookbooks, lavender, housewares and gifts. The packaged sets of olive oils and vinegars are particularly nice and make great gifts.

OPEN DAILY
10am-5pm

Olive Oil Tasting Bar

Vinegars

Gourmet Foods

Housewares

V, MC, AE, DC

Owner:
Peggy O'Kelly

OAKVILLE
RUTHERFORD

The retail room also serves an educational purpose. Tours and tasting sessions may be arranged, and there are frequently seminars or lectures. Get on the mailing list!

TOP OAKVILLE PICNIC SPOTS
PICNIC ETIQUETTE: BUY WINE FROM THE HOST WINERY

LA FAMIGLIA • CHATEAU POTELLE

LA FAMIGLIA WINERY

Closed Tues-Wed
Th-M: 10am-4:30pm
1595 Oakville Grade
(888) 453-9463
(707) 968-2364

Tasting fee: $5
Bottles start at $20

CHATEAU POTELLE

Closed Tues-Wed
Th-M: 11am-5pm
3875 Mt Veeder Road
(707) 255-9440

No Tasting Fee
Reserve Tasting: $5
Bottles start at $14

LA FAMIGLIA di ROBERT MONDAVI Located just a few miles up Oakville Grade, La Famiglia Winery is easy to get to and high enough to have spectacular views. Picnic tables on a tree-shaded deck overlook the valley to the mountains beyond. Visitors are welcome to play bocce ball (they'll even lend you the balls), but it's a good idea to reserve ahead. Try one of La Famiglia's Italian varietals: Sangiovese, Pinot Grigio, Barbera, Colmera or Moscato Bianco.

CHATEAU POTELLE is a mountain-top winery with views that are to die for. Getting there is a time commitment, easily half an hour from Hwy 29. Two-lane roads, hairpin turns, and gorgeous scenery are guaranteed to exhilarate or terrify you, but when you finally reach the top, the breathtaking 360-degree view is the payoff. Potelle makes Chardonnay, Sauvignon Blanc, Zinfandel, and Cabernet wines and was named one the outstanding American Wineries by *Wine & Spirits* magazine in 2001.

The 2003 Robert Mondavi Summer Music Festival schedule will be announced in late April.. Picnic on the lawn before the show. Call 888-766-6328 in late April for details.

TOP RUTHERFORD PICNIC SPOTS
PICNIC ETIQUETTE: CHECK IN WITH THE TASTING ROOM

SEQUOIA GROVE • RUTHERFORD GROVE

SEQUOIA GROVE VINEYARDS – Down on the valley floor, a rustic 100-year-old farmhouse surrounded by some of the last sequoia redwood trees in Napa Valley is a grand centerpiece and logo for this family winery. Outside the tasting room, a pretty garden patio with bistro tables and chairs and lots of shade serves as the picnic area. Sequoia Grove produces Chardonnay and Cabernet Sauvignon wines, as well as Allen Family Shiraz and Gerwürztraminer.

SEQUOIA GROVE

Open Daily
10:30am-5pm
8338 St. Helena Hwy
(707) 944-2945

Tasting Fee: $5
Bottles start at $12

RUTHERFORD GROVE WINERY – This wonderful picnic spot is one of the upper valley's better-kept secrets. Conveniently located off Hwy 29 (just south of Galleron Road), but far enough away to eliminate most road noise, this family-run winery is nestled in a lovely grove of 100-year-old eucalyptus trees. All the picnic tables on the shaded lawn behind the tasting room have gorgeous views of the surrounding vineyards. Rutherford Grove produces Merlot, Cabernet, Sangiovese, Chardonnay and Riesling wines, as well Napa Valley Grapeseed Oil, a healthy source of Vitamin E and omega-6.

RUTHERFORD GROVE

Open Daily
10am-4:30pm
1673 St. Helena Hwy
(707) 963-0544

Tasting fee: $3
Reserve wines: $5
Bottles start at $12

OAKVILLE RUTHERFORD

Sequoia Grove hosts a Summer Music Festival one Sunday a month June through September. The concert is free, picnicking is welcome, and regular wine tasting is complimentary.

TOP RUTHERFORD AREA PICNIC SPOTS
PICNIC ETIQUETTE: BUY WINE FROM THE HOST WINERY

RUTHERFORD HILL• NICHELINI • CATACULA LAKE

RUTHERFORD HILL
Open Daily
10am-5pm
200 Rutherford Hill Rd
(707) 963-1871
Tasting Fee: $5
Bottles start at $14

RUTHERFORD HILL WINERY is just yards up the hill from Auberge du Soleil. You get exactly the same view with none of the expense. Picnic tables are scattered throughout an olive grove, some more level than others, but who cares, with THAT view?

NICHELINI WINERY
Open Sa-Su only
Summer:10am-6pm
Winter: 10am-5pm
2950 Sage Canyon Rd
(707) 963-0717
No Tasting Fee
Bottles start at $12

NICHELINI WINERY is the "oldest family-run winery in Napa Valley." Anton Nichelini homesteaded here in 1884, and now 3rd generation Nichelinis are making wine from grapes grown in nearby Chiles Valley. There are bocce ball courts and lots of picnic tables on multiple levels.

CATACULA LAKE
Open Wed-Mon
By Appt Only
11am-3:30pm
4105 Chiles Pope
Valley Road
(707) 965-1104
No Tasting Fee
Bottles start at $11

CATACULA LAKE WINERY may be only a 15-minute drive from Silverado Trail, but it's worlds away from the Napa Valley most people see, and well worth a special trip. This is back-road country with rolling hills and gorgeous vistas, horse ranches and vineyards. Many say this is the way Napa Valley looked 40 years ago. Enjoy a picnic next to the winery's private lake and see for yourself. Just call ahead to make sure someone's there!

A favorite scenic loop drive passes both Nichelini and Catacula Lake wineries. Take Hwy 128 to Lower Chiles Pope Valley Road, to Chiles Pope Valley Road, then back to Hwy 128.

RUTHERFORD NITE LIFE

AUBERGE DU SOLEIL • RUTHERFORD GRILL

AUBERGE DU SOLEIL is the best spot in the immediate area for a nightcap or a late snack. Everything about this 5-star establishment is top-notch, and the bar is no exception. A creative and and delicious bar menu is served until 11pm nightly.

AUBERGE DU SOLEIL
180 Rutherford Hill Rd
(707) 963-1211
Open Nightly

Bar Hours:
11am-11pm

The RUTHERFORD GRILL is the only other choice with late hours, but only on Friday and Saturday, when the bar stays open until 10:30pm with full menu service. On weeknights they're open until 9:30pm.

RUTHERFORD GRILL
1180 Rutherford Rd
(707) 963-1792

SEE THE OAKVILLE • RUTHERFORD RESTAURANT SECTION (pp. 93, 95) FOR COMPLETE INFORMATION ON BOTH THESE SPOTS.

Rutherford's Beaulieu Vineyards was founded in 1900 by George La Tour. Prohibition put most wineries out of business, but BV stayed alive selling altar wine to the Catholic Church!

Notes

St. Helena

St. Helena Farmers Market

St. Helena

Founded in 1857, St. Helena is home to some of the most famous wineries in the world. Many of the winery buildings are architectural gems more than 100 years old and are now on the National Register of Historic Places. Beringer's Rhine House, Charles Krug's Carriage House, and the former Christian Brothers Winery (now the Culinary Institute of America) were all built between 1881 and 1889 and are wonderful examples of vastly different architectural styles.

Historic Main Street is also a treat, with original façades dating back to the late 1800's. The downtown area is very compact, so park your car on one of the side streets and explore St. Helena on foot. You'll be amazed at how many fine shops and restaurants are located within just a few blocks. Whether shopping for art (be sure to visit the galleries), fine jewelry, antiques, gifts, clothes or furniture, you will find it all right here.

Spend some time exploring the back streets, where you will find the *Napa Valley Olive Oil Manufacturing Company*, just down the street from *Tra Vigne*, on Charter Oak. Filled to the brim with olive oil, cheese, pasta, sausages, and all the other foodstuffs necessary for an authentic Italian meal, "The Olive Oil

Factory," as it's known to locals, is a Napa Valley institution. Hundreds of yellowed business cards left by visitors cover the ceiling and the walls and give you a sense of how long this place has been around, and how popular it is! History buffs will want to visit the highly acclaimed Silverado Museum next to the local library a couple of blocks off Main Street. This tiny museum dedicated entirely to the life and works of Robert Louis Stevenson is filled with original writings and artifacts related to this famous American author.

If sports are in your plans, rent a bike from St. Helena Cyclery and take a ride out to historic White Sulphur Springs Inn & Spa, or head to the horseback riding stables north of town next to Bothe-Napa Valley State Park. If you are staying at Meadowood Resort, try a game of croquet on the world-class lawns or pick up a game of golf or tennis. If you have your own equipment, you're welcome to play Bocce ball or tennis for free at beautiful Crane Park.

Although St. Helena is home to many restaurants that make dining an art form, you can also find terrific casual dining spots like *Taylor's Refresher* for hamburgers and shakes. On Friday mornings from May to October, people flock to the *St. Helena Farmers Market* in Crane Park. Considered one of the top Farmers Markets in the U.S., this is a slice of Americana not to be missed.

If you still have energy left in the evening, take in a movie at the *Cameo Cinema*, or enjoy live music at *1351 Lounge*.

ST. HELENA KEY

ST. HELENA

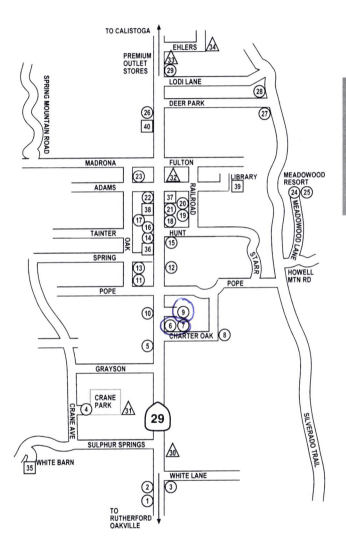

Notes

ADVENTURES IN DINING

ARMADILLO'S
1304 Main Street • St. Helena • (707) 963-8082

MEXICAN

It's always fiesta time at *Armadillo's* thanks to the rainbow-colored tables, glass mosaic tiles and vibrant murals on the walls. For eleven years now, Chef/owner Tony Velasquez has been putting a "fresh Californian-Mexican" spin on traditional favorites, as well as creating his own signature dishes like the popular chingalinga (shredded chicken and cheese rolled in a flour tortilla and deep fried) and spinach quesadilla. There are always several daily specials in addition to the main menu. Absolutely everything is fresh and made from scratch, right down to the potato and tortilla chips! If you're looking for a late breakfast or brunch, the Huevos Rancheros ($7.25) and Chorizo con Huevos ($8.25) can be ordered all day long. A few red and white California wines are available by the glass along with a good selection of Mexican beers. The reasonable prices and consistently friendly service make this a favorite with locals.

CLOSED TUESDAYS

HOURS
Su, M, W, Th:
11am-9pm
F-Sa: 11am-10pm

Appetizers: $4-$10
Entrées: $6-$12
Desserts: $2-$4

Continuous Dining
Corkage: $5
Reservations: No

V, MC
Locals' Favorite
Family Friendly
Catering
Takeout

Chef:
Tony Velasquez

Amardillo's Margaritas are made with a special tequila that is only 20% alcohol (in compliance with their liquor license!). Try one – they're very tasty.

GILLWOOD'S CAFÉ
1313 Main Street • St. Helena • (707) 963-1788

AMERICAN

OPEN DAILY

BREAKFAST:
7am-3pm
Prices: $4-$9

LUNCH:
11:30am-3pm
Prices: $4-$10
Desserts: $3-$4

Hamburgers

Continuous Dining

No Alcohol

Reservations: No

V, MC, AE

Locals' Favorite

Family Friendly

Takeout

Located in the heart of St. Helena, *Gillwood's* is the most popular breakfast spot in town, opening much earlier than anyplace else. Traditional breakfast fare is served until 3pm daily. Lunch selections include excellent soups sandwiches and salads. Casual and friendly, most of the wait staff have worked here for years; you'll probably recognize a couple of them depicted in the huge oil painting hanging on the wall. Daily specials featuring seasonal fruits and vegetables posted on boards hanging above the counter should not be missed even if the waiters don't mention them. The homemade bakery items are particularly good. Nothing is especially fancy or trendy here, just good, home-style cooking. Things get really busy on weekend mornings, so try one of two recommended approaches to avoid waiting: either get there before 8:30am, or call ahead, ask for the expected wait time and get your name on the list. A community table near the entrance often has immediate seating for small parties.

Instead of toast with your breakfast, substitute a homemade muffin for no additional charge. Varieties are posted next to the specials. The raspberry streusel muffin is incredible.

GREEN VALLEY CAFÉ
1310 Main Street • St. Helena • (707) 963-7088

ITALIAN

Look for the red half curtains at the windows and the green awning over the doorway, and you'll have found this tiny trattoria specializing in Northern Italian cuisine. The dining room is long and very narrow, with tables so close together you'll need to inhale just to get through. Don't think of it as crowded, think of it as friendly, because friendly is the operative word here, applying equally to the owners, staff, food, and fellow diners. It's virtually impossible NOT to have a conversation with your neighbor! While the pasta dishes are all terrific, the gnocchi, lasagna and cannelloni (a frequent special) are divine. Try sharing an order of the calamari fritti ($13.75) as an appetizer, or if Italian "comfort" food rings your chimes, order the braised lamb shank with polenta ($17). Always check the blackboard for daily food and wine specials. The full menu is also served at the bar. *Green Valley's* moderately priced wine list features 40-50 California and Italian wines. It's easy to see why this little gem is a favorite with locals!

CLOSED SUN-MON

LUNCH:
11:30am-3pm
Appetizers: $5-$8
Entrées: $12-$14
Desserts: $4-$6

DINNER:
5:30pm-9:30pm
Appetizers: $6-$8
Entrées: $12-$20
Desserts: $6-$8

Corkage: $10
Reservations: Yes

V, MC

Locals' Favorite
Takeout

Chef:
Cherie & Delio
Cuneo

ST. HELENA

Waiting for your table? Have a cocktail at the upscale bar across the street, 1351 Lounge. Let Green Valley know that's where you're headed – they'll call when your table is ready.

MARTINI HOUSE
1245 Spring Street • St. Helena • (707) 963-2233

CALIFORNIA

OPEN DAILY

LUNCH:
11:30pm-3pm
Appetizers: $8-$13
Entrées: $14-$22
Desserts: $8

DINNER:
5:30pm-10pm
Appetizers: $11-$20
Entrées: $20-$36
Desserts: $8

Wine Bar
Winning Wine List
Corkage: $20
Reservations: Yes

V, MC, AE, DC
Romantic Spot
Locals' Favorite
Bay Area Top 100
Special Events
Chef:
Todd Humphries

Named for the original owner and bootlegger, *not* the drink, Pat Kuleto's new restaurant is not only gorgeous, the food is divine. No expense was spared in restoring this 1923 Craftsman bungalow-turned-restaurant. An impressive stone fireplace, dark wood and oversized upholstered chairs create a handsome, "private club" atmosphere in the main dining room. Full flavors and a refined "heartiness" characterize menu items like roasted mushroom soup, pork chops, duck, steak and venison. A more casual air prevails in the *Wine Cellar Bar* downstairs, a favorite with locals, where seating is first come, first served. Outdoor seating in the garden is possible much of the year under the arbor or around the fountain. At lunchtime, opt for the 3-course prix fixe menu, reasonably priced at $20. *Martini House's* wine list is one of the Valley's most ambitious with 600 local and international selections, and it is known for its consumer friendly approach to wine classifications. Reservations are a must in the upstairs dining room and outside.

An afternoon menu ("light bites") is served from 3pm-5pm in the Wine Cellar Bar and on the patio. And yes, the Martinis are fantastic!

MIRAMONTE RESTAURANT & CAFÉ
1327 Railroad Avenue • St. Helena • (707) 963-1200

CALIFORNIA

Mustards maven Cindy Pawlcyn's latest Napa Valley venture, the Latin-inspired *Miramonte* in downtown St. Helena, opened in Spring 2001. Splashy window boxes add color to the whitewashed stucco exterior of the circa 1850 building. Upstairs the expansive, light-filled dining room has exposed beams and a vaulted ceiling. Downstairs, the look is sunny and crisp, with colorful artwork decorating the white walls. A small but charming patio area under an ancient fig tree is a great spot for lunch. True to form, Pawlcyn changes the menu seasonally, favoring local bounty from the many growers and producers in the area. The food is characterized as "cuisine of the Americas," with South and Central American influences clearly evident in many of the specialty dishes prepared by Chef de Cuisine/Partner Pablo Jacinto. The Stuffed Pasilla Chile with Pablo's mother-in-law's mole, black beans and rice is a good example. The wine list is especially fun, including wines from Chile, Mexico and Argentina as well as California and Oregon.

OPEN DAILY
LUNCH / DINNER:
Su-Th:
11:30am-9:30pm
F-Sa:
11:30am-10pm
Appetizers: $5-$11
Entrées: $10-$26
Desserts: $6-$7

Hamburgers (lunch)
Continuous Dining

Wine Bar
Winning Wine List
Corkage: $12
Reservations: Yes

V, MC, AE, DC
Special Events
Catering
Takeout

Chef: Pablo Jacinto,
Cindy Pawlcyn

The Latin inspiration continues at the bar. Try a Mojito (Havana Rum with mint) or Brazil's popular Caiparinha, made with Cachaca, a whole chopped lime and cane syrup.

PINOT BLANC
641 Main Street • St. Helena • (707) 963-6191

CALIFORNIA

OPEN DAILY

LUNCH:
11:30am-3pm
Appetizers: $8-$13
Entrées: $17-$24
Desserts: $6-$8

DINNER:
5pm-9:30pm
Appetizers: $8-$13
Entrées: $17-$24
Desserts: $6-$8

Hamburgers (Lunch)
Winning Wine List
Corkage: $15
Reservations: Yes

V, MC, AE, DC
Special Events
Catering
Takeout

Chef: Sean Knight

A member of the Patina Group of restaurants well known in Southern California and Las Vegas, *Pinot Blanc* is the company's only Northern California location. Several years ago, a radical facelift gave the restaurant a whole new and much improved look. Dark woods were lightened and the generous use of soft yellows, whites and red accents create an open, airy feeling. *Pinot Blanc's* bar is one of the nicest in town, ideal for a pre-dinner drink or meeting with friends. Out back, a large, tree-shaded patio with an enormous fireplace is a welcome oasis from the hustle and bustle of Hwy 29. Executive Chef Sean Knight's classic California cuisine takes full advantage of locally grown meat, poultry, and produce. An excellent variety of fresh fish, locally raised lamb and duck are regularly featured. The luncheon menu is perfect for lighter appetites and features a terrific salad nicoise with seared ahi tuna. The 300+ wine list is impressive. Feel free to have a look in the wine cellar behind the bar.

Wednesday night is Local's Night with a special prix fixe dinner for only $28. In the summertime, it's a 3-course BBQ. Pssst! You don't really have to be a local to come.

ROUX

1234 Main Street • St. Helena • (707) 963-5330

CALIFORNIA

Surrender immediately to owners Vincent and Tyla Nattress, and the entire experience at *Roux* will be an intimate one, beginning with the coziness of decor to the "let us cook for you" concept of the carefully crafted tasting menu. Everything on the menu may be ordered à la carte, but the 4-course prix fixe tasting menu is a 5-star experience. Chef Vincent Nattress trained under Hiro Sone at *Terra* and exhibits that same meticulous attention to culinary detail, from the extraordinary combination of flavors to the exquisite presentation. Each course is a unique taste experience, so choosing one perfect wine can be difficult. Wine impresario Tyla Nattress solves that problem with "let us pair for you," selecting a different wine for each course to complement and enhance the subtleties of the food. This option is an additional $27 per person, and worth every penny -- not just for the lesson in pairing, but for the superb quality of the wines served. The wine list may be short, but it's impressive: less than 1,000 cases of each selection were produced.

CLOSED SUN-MON

DINNER:
5:30pm-10pm
Appetizers: $8-$13
Entrées: $19-$24
Desserts: $5-$7

Prix Fixe: $45
Wine Pairing: $27

Wine Bar
Winning Wine List
Corkage: $15
Reservations: Yes

V, MC, AE
Romantic Spot
Bay Area To 100
Special Events
Catering

Chefs/Owners:
Vincent & Tyla
Nattress

Each night Roux offers several exceptional (and hard-to-find) wines by the glass. They also have an impressive list of rare ports and dessert wines.

SILVERADO BREWING COMPANY
3020 N. St. Helena Hwy • St. Helena • (707) 967-9876

AMERICAN

ST. HELENA

OPEN DAILY

LUNCH / DINNER:
Su-Th: 4:30pm-9pm
F-Sa: 11:30am-10pm
Appetizers: $3-$9
Entrées: $5-$19
Desserts: $4-$6

Hamburgers
Brewpub
Continuous Dining
Corkage: None
Reservations: Yes

V, MC, AE
Nite Life
Locals' Favorite
Family Friendly
Special Events
Catering
Takeout

Chef:
Bernard Ayala

Anyone beginning to whine about too much wine? In the historic building adjacent to Freemark Abbey lies concrete proof that another beverage of choice is alive and well: beer. Completely remodeled in 1995, the atmosphere at this brewpub/restaurant is casual and cozy, with high ceilings and lots of exposed stone. On full display behind the glass partition at the end of the bar, the brewing operation produces four standard and two special beers daily. They also brew their own root beer and cream soda! Everything on the menu is either made with beer, such as the beer battered Fish 'n' Chips, or is designed to go with beer, like the slow-roasted prime rib or Flat Iron Steak. For lighter appetites, there is a very good selection of appetizers and salad entrées. Beer may the specialty of the house, but enophiles need not fret. The wine list is quite good, offering more than 50 wines from local vintners.

Silverado Brewing has a large bar, with tables, dance floor and live entertainment every Friday and Saturday night until 10pm.

TAYLOR'S REFRESHER
933 Main Street • St. Helena • (707) 963-3486

AMERICAN

Taylor's is a 1950's-style drive-in on Main Street that has been a St. Helena institution for generations. When Joel and Duncan Gott bought *Taylor's* in the late 1990's, they gave it a major facelift worthy of an Oscar before reopening in 1999. These culinary entrepreneurs cut their teeth at the family's *Palisades Market* in Calistoga, and the same brand of innovation is clearly evident at *Taylor's*. Large, juicy burgers with secret sauce, fresh-cut fries and super-thick shakes may be the big draw, but you'll also find gourmet roadside specialties including fish and chips using fresh halibut, seared ahi burgers, plus a few kid pleasers (corn dogs and grilled cheese). Even the shakes have style! Try espresso bean or white pistachio for a delicious change. Several wines are available by the glass or half bottle, along with draft beers. Order at the counter, then find a seat beneath the covered area (heated during the winter months), or at one of the shaded picnic tables on the lawn. Avoid waiting by calling in your order. Then head straight to the pick-up window.

OPEN DAILY

Summer: 11am-9pm
Winter: 11am-8pm

Hamburgers: $5-$9
Sandwiches: $3-$12

Continuous Dining
Corkage: $5

Reservations: No

V, MC, AE

Locals' Favorite

Family Friendly

Takeout

Owners:
Joel & Duncan Gott

Joel Gott also happens to make a Zinfandel under his own name that is pretty fabulous. You can find it at Dean & Deluca in St. Helena and Palisades Market in Calistoga.

ST. HELENA

TERRA
1345 Railroad Avenue • St. Helena • (707) 963-8931

FUSION

CLOSED TUESDAYS

Weekdays: 6pm-9pm
Fri-Su: 6pm-10pm

Appetizers: $10-$15
Entrées: $19-$29
Desserts: $7-$8

Winning Wine List
Corkage: $20
Reservations: Yes

V, MC, DC
Romantic Spot
Locals' Favorite
Bay Area Top 100

Chefs/Owners:
Hiro Sone &
Lissa Doumani

For virtually all of its fifteen years, *Terra* has received accolades as one of the best restaurants in the Bay Area. It is also one of the most beautiful. Built entirely of fieldstone nearly a century ago, the rock walls are fully exposed inside and out. The elegant ambience of this intimate restaurant is mirrored in the food prepared by chef/owners Hiro Sone and Lissa Doumani. This husband and wife team met in 1983 while both were chefs at *Spago* in Los Angeles. Their signature style reflects their individual tastes and histories: Hiro's imaginative dishes contain traces of his Japanese ancestry as well as classical training in Italian and French cuisine, and Lissa's pastries and desserts are legendary. Her long-standing roots in the Napa Valley combined with her Lebanese heritage make her the ideal hospitality manager. If you love special cookbooks, check out their recently published *Terra: Cooking from the Heart of the Napa Valley.*

Let them know in advance if you are celebrating a special occasion. They'll be sure to make it memorable and even personalize the menu as a keepsake.

THE GRILL AT MEADOWOOD
900 Meadowood Lane • St. Helena • (707) 963-3646

CALIFORNIA

If you're not a guest at Meadowood Resort, dining at one of their two restaurants is the next best thing. Sporty and casual, with a clubhouse atmosphere, *The Grill* serves breakfast, lunch and dinner. Every seat in the house enjoys an idyllic view overlooking the 9-hole golf course and perfectly manicured croquet lawns. The eclectic menu is exactly what you would expect at a world-class resort. Sandwiches, salads, fresh fish, roasted chicken, steak, pork tenderloin, and a fantastic ground sirloin hamburger (try it with blue cheese!) are always on the menu. Breakfast is outstanding, especially the delicious croissant French toast with raisins soaked in Cointreau. Heart-healthy and calorie-counted "Spa Cuisine" selections are also available. One of the great pleasures of visiting *The Grill* is the exceedingly friendly and helpful staff, who go well beyond your normal expectations in accommodating special orders or dietary needs. *The Grill* and *The Restaurant* share the same exceptional wine list.

OPEN DAILY
BREAKFAST:
7am-11:30am
Prices: $5-$12
LUNCH:
11:30am-3:30pm
Prices: $9-$16
BAR MENU
3:30pm-5:30pm
DINNER:
5:30pm-10pm
Appetizers: $11-$20
Entrées: $20-$36
Desserts: $8

Hamburgers
Winning Wine List
Corkage: $15
Reservations: Yes

V, MC, AE, DC
Family Friendly
Special Events
Catering
Executive Chef:
Didier Lenders

ST. HELENA

At the very least, enjoy a lemonade or a cocktail on the terrace of The Grill. Towering pines and the surrounding hills make this an incredibly beautiful and unique destination.

THE RESTAURANT AT MEADOWOOD
900 Meadowood Lane • St. Helena • (707) 963-3646

CALIFORNIA

ST. HELENA

OPEN DAILY

DINNER:
Su-Th: 6pm-9:30pm
Fri-Sa: 6pm-10pm

Appetizers: $9-$25
Entrées: $30-$36
Desserts: $8-$10

Vintners Menu
$125 (with wine)
4-Course Prix Fixe
$65 (without wine)

Sunday Brunch
(April-October)

Winning Wine List
Corkage: $15
Reservations: Yes

V, MC, AE, DC
Romantic Spot
Special Events
Chef: Steven Tevere

The Restaurant is open for evening "fine dining" year-round and Sunday Brunch during high season. Dramatic and elegant with a soaring cathedral ceiling and exposed beams, the dining room enjoys expansive views of the golf course, croquet lawns and surrounding hills. Chef Steven Tevere's creative California cuisine may be ordered à la carte, as a 4-course prix fixe, or 6-course "Vintners Menu" paired with wines. A wonderful choice for that special occasion or celebration, service is attentive and unhurried, while preparation and presentation are consistently top-notch. The menu is a quick lesson in Wine Country premium producers and purveyors of fine foods: Petaluma Veal, Sonoma Foie Gras, Goats Leap Goat Cheese, Wolf Farm Squab, Superior Farms Lamb, and the list goes on. In winter, take the chill off by enjoying a cocktail or aperitif in front of the large stone fireplace in the bar.

No description of Meadowood is complete without mentioning the wine list, one of the most extensive collections of Napa Valley wines in the world.

Meadowood wine guru, John Thoreen, is available for tasting classes, parties, and other custom wine experiences that can be tailored to all levels of wine enthusiasm (and knowledge)!

TRA VIGNE
1050 Charter Oak • St. Helena • (707) 963-4444

ITALIAN

This has been a favorite restaurant with locals and tourists for 15 years for three reasons: outstanding food, delightful ambience, and exceptional service. *Tra Vigne* chefs often go on to great things, as evidenced by founding chef Michael Chiarello, but not before mentoring their successors to carry on the standard of excellence. Talented Executive Chef Michael Reardon is currently at the helm. A feast for the eye as well as the palate, the spacious and elegant dining room lies just beyond the theatrical drapes in the foyer. Doors at one end of the room open onto a covered terrace for outdoor dining, and a stunning hand-carved bar dominates the other end. The tree-shaded courtyard, shared by the *Cantinetta*, is lovely for lunch, or cocktails at night. Serving continuously throughout the day, lunch and dinner menus are identical. It's impossible to go wrong here, but the Baked Pecorino Cheese Pudding appetizer and Pesce Arrosto (roasted whole fish, usually snapper or bass), are to die for. The international wine list is fabulous.

OPEN DAILY

LUNCH / DINNER:
11:30am-10:30pm
Appetizers: $7-$13
Entrées: $15-$33
Desserts: $4-$7

Continuous Dining
Late Kitchen
Wine Bar
Winning Wine List
Corkage: $15
Reservations: Yes

V, MC
Locals' Favorite
Special Events
Catering
Takeout

Chef:
Michael Reardon

One of Tra Vigne's fabulous martinis makes the inevitable wait more palatable, or try one of the 100+ wines by the glass at the Cantinetta, in the courtyard.

VILLA CORONA - ST. HELENA
1138 Main Street • St. Helena • (707) 963-7812

MEXICAN

OPEN DAILY

BREAKFAST:
M-F 10am-11am
Sa-Su 10am-Noon

LUNCH / DINNER:
Mon: 11am-2:30pm
Tu-Sat: 11am-8pm
Su: 11am-5pm
Prices: $3-$10

Continuous Dining
Corkage: None
Reservations: No

V, MC, DC
Locals' Favorite
Family Friendly

Catering
Takeout

We just love this casual eatery for its delicious food, friendly service, and reasonable prices. If you're looking for authentic preparations of Mexico's most popular dishes, head to *Villa Corona* where the usual favorites join hard-to-find goodies like flautas and camarones (prawns) on the menu. Carnitas fans will love the tender, lean pork, with just the right amount of crispiness. The home-made tortillas are outstanding. There's nothing fancy here: Place your order at the counter and have a seat; you'll be served tableside by the young, enthusiastic wait staff. The décor is simple and distinctly southwestern; with lacquered wood tables and ladder-back chairs ideal for family style dining, plus a few café tables on the sidewalk. *Villa Corona* is one of the few St. Helena restaurants serving breakfast daily from 10am-11am M-F, and 10am-Noon on weekends. No omelets or French toast, just great eggs and chorizo, tortilla wraps, and huevos rancheros. A variety of Mexican beer is available and wine may be brought in with NO corkage fee.

Service is always efficient here, making it a perfect spot to grab an early dinner before catching a movie down the street at another of our favorite spots, the Cameo Cinema.

VITTE
1020 Main Street • St. Helena • (707) 967-9999

ITALIAN

Vitte is the remodeled and slightly upscale version of the popular *Tomatina*, adjoining the Inn at Southbridge on Main Street. It's easy to miss: Only a small sign on Hwy 29 directs you across the railroad tracks to the large red tomato marking the entrance. Pizza remains the main attraction, but more pasta dishes, sandwiches and salads have been added. Nothing is over $14, and ordering at the counter has been eliminated in favor of table service. The industrial look is gone: roomy leather booths now line two ends of the room, with lots of tables of all sizes in the center. *Vitte* can easily accommodate multiple large parties as well as groups of 2 and 4, with additional seating on the patio. The new, pressed tin barrel ceiling over the dining room is beautiful and functional, greatly reducing the decibel level, and indirect lighting, creamy colors and earth tones create a very inviting atmosphere. The large bar area still contains a big-screen TV and pool table. At least 25 inexpensive to moderately priced wines are available by the glass or bottle.

OPEN DAILY

LUNCH / DINNER:
Su-Th:
11:30am-9:30pm
F-Sa:
11:30am-10pm

Appetizers: $3-$7
Entrées: $7-13
Desserts: $4-$5
Pizza: $10-$20

Continuous Dining
Wine Bar
Corkage: None
Reservations: No
(unless 8 or more)

V, MC, DC

Family Friendly

Takeout

Vitte is a rare combination of reasonable prices, great atmosphere and good food, easily accommodating groups of all sizes. Reservations can be made for parties of 8 or more.

ST. HELENA

WINE SPECTATOR GREYSTONE
2555 Main Street • St. Helena • (707) 967-1010

CALIFORNIA

ST. HELENA

OPEN DAILY

LUNCH / DINNER:
Su-Th: 11:30am-9pm
F-Sa: 11:30am-10pm
Appetizers: $6-$11
Entrées: $15-$28
Desserts: $5-$7

Continuous Dining
Winning Wine List
Corkage: $15
Reservations: Yes

V, MC, AE, DC

Catering

Takeout

Chef: Pilar Sanchez

Originally built in 1889 as the Christian Brothers Winery, this imposing stone masterpiece was saved from demolition by the Culinary Institute of America and given new life as their West Coast campus. *Wine Spectator Greystone* is named in honor of the magazine's owner and CIA benefactor, Marvin Shanken. If you haven't eaten here recently, it's time for a return visit. Chef Pilar Sanchez completely revamped the menu: the "tapas"-style Mediterranean menu has been replaced with classic California Cuisine featuring fish, meat, poultry, and vegetarian selections. The baskets of brick oven breads are incredible (buy one to take home for $6). The decor is "industrial chic," with concrete floors, high ceilings, and colorful furniture arranged around an enormous "show kitchen," allowing diners to view the chefs from every angle. Valley views are limited to warm weather, when a few outdoor tables have views of Charles Krug Vineyards and the surrounding mountains. As you would expect with a namesake like this one, the all-California

Be sure to save some time for a visit to the CIA, where you can take a tour, enjoy a cooking demonstration or just check out the campus store. It's worth seeing.

ADVENTURES IN DINING

CANTINETTA DELICATESSEN & WINE BAR
1050 Charter Oak • St. Helena • (707) 963-8888

DELI & RESTAURANT • WINE SHOP

Located in the courtyard of *Tra Vigne*, *Cantinetta* is the perfect place to stock the picnic basket, have an informal lunch or light dinner. Chef Mariano Orlando, author of numerous cookbooks, focuses on his native Sicilian cuisine. Hot and cold sandwiches stuffed with Italian meats, cheese, or vegetables are served on fresh baked bread or focaccia. Pizzas, salads, lemon herb chicken, and asparagus tart are regularly featured. The tiny store is lined with wine bottles and a large wine bar serves 100+ premium and hard-to-find "cult" wines by the glass. The list averages $2 to $7.50 for a 2-ounce taste and $5 to $10 for 5 ounces, on up. The main menu is served until 5pm, but "Boconcini per Vini" are available until closing. These "little bites for wine" are small portions of bruschetta, cheese, meats, or smoked salmon for $2.50 per plate. Sunday Night Wine Tastings, 6pm-8pm, feature a local winemaker who chats and pours. These Sunday Night Wine Tastings are free, and extremely popular with locals.

OPEN DAILY

LUNCH / DINNER
11:30am-5pm
Prices: $4-$7

"LITTLE BITES"
5pm-10pm
Prices: $2.50/plate

Wine Bar
Winning Wine List
Corkage: None
Reservations: No

V, MC, DC
Locals' Favorite
Special Events
Catering

Chef:
Mariano Orlando

Take a cooking class from Mariano Orlando at the Napa Valley College campus in St. Helena as part of the Community Education series. Call (707) 967-2900 to request a schedule.

GIUGNI'S DELICATESSEN
1227 Main Street • St. Helena • (707) 963-3421

DELI & RESTAURANT

ST. HELENA

OPEN DAILY

HOURS: 9am-4:55pm

Sandwiches: $4-$6

No alcohol

Reservations: No

Cash Only

If only walls could talk! The well-worn, creaky wooden floor is your first tip off: *Giugni's* has been doing it their way for a long, long time. Signs in the window alert passers-by to significant events like birthdays, graduations or new babies. Old newspaper articles, favorite jokes, and photographs taped to the walls pass for artwork. Ambience aside, you won't get a better sandwich anywhere. Head to the rear of the store to the display case and grab a menu. Choose among two dozen meats (including every kind of salami imaginable), over a dozen cheeses and a variety of breads, crusty rolls, or foccacia. Sprouts, lettuce, red onion and tomato are all standard equipment along with the famous Giugni Juice (a secret blend of vinegar, oil and spices). For a treat, add extras like avocado, cranberries, cucumbers, or bacon. There are also salads, soft drinks, chips, homemade brownies and cookies. Inside seating is available in the back room. They open at 9am daily. This is NOT a breakfast place, but sandwiches can be picked up bright and early.

Giugni's gets very busy at lunchtime. Avoid standing in line by phoning in your sandwich order. A menu isn't mandatory-you want it, chances are they've got it.

V. SATTUI WINERY DELICATESSEN
1111 White Lane • St. Helena • (707) 963-7774

DELI • PICNIC AREA

Driving into St Helena from the south, it's impossible to miss the hordes of people crowding the *V. Sattui Winery* picnic area immediately adjacent to Highway 29. Some say it's because of the wine, others say it's because of the cheese . . . and salami, and sandwiches, and the list goes on. Don't be put off by the crowds. Getting through the deli is not difficult, and the excellent selection of casual picnic fare makes it worthwhile. *V. Sattui's* cheese selection rivals *Dean & DeLuca's*, and the prepared foods are outstanding. Gulf shrimp, pastas, and numerous salads are made daily. In addition to food stuffs, the deli area has an excellent assortment of picnic-related items such as outfitted baskets and wine coolers. Needless to say, *V. Sattui* wines are the only ones available for purchase on site. When you're ready to have your picnic, arm wrestling for a table and inhaling exhaust fumes are strictly optional: there are a number of fabulous picnic spots within a short drive. Check Top Picnic Spots on pp139-140 for suggestions.

OPEN DAILY

HOURS: 9am-6pm

Picnic Area

V, MC

ST. HELENA

V. Sattui's gift shop is terrific. You'll find pottery, glassware, linens, picnic gear, home accessories plus a boat load of wine-related merchandise.

DEAN & DELUCA MARKET
607 S. St Helena Hwy • St. Helena • (707) 967-9980

DELI • PRODUCE • HOUSEWARES • WINE

ST. HELENA

OPEN DAILY

STORE HOURS:
9am-7pm

ESPRESSO BAR
Opens 7:30am
Pastries: $3-$4

Winning Wine Shop

V, MC, AE

Catering

The Big Apple finally took a bite out of Napa Valley when *Dean & DeLuca* came to town a few years ago. As the sole DDL store on the West Coast, this Wine Country magnet is a "must-stop" for tourists. You'll find an espresso bar, gourmet foods, kitchenware, and an enormous wine shop. The Espresso Bar opens at 7:30am daily, with arguably the best selection of breakfast pastries in town. The main store doesn't open until 9am, but no one objects to you wandering around, coffee in hand. All department managers are impresarios in their fields, so if you're overwhelmed by the number of pâtés, or wondering if the caviar for $100 is really that much better than the one for $40, ask away. The cheese department is extraordinary, with over 300 varieties. Ask for a recommendation; you'll get an education. The same can be said of the outstanding Wine Department. *Dean & DeLuca* is not just a store, it's an experience.

A great place for people watching! The limos coming and going are especially entertaining--who knew they made stretch humvees and PT Cruisers?

NAPA VALLEY OLIVE OIL MFG. CO.
835 Charter Oak • St. Helena • (707) 963-4173

DELI • ITALIAN GROCERY • OLIVE OIL

Owned and operated by the Lucchesi and Particelli families since 1930, *"The Olive Oil Factory"* is the real deal. You're as likely to hear Italian spoken as English while browsing around this funky, historic building. Although the olive oil production was relocated to the Upper Sacramento Valley years ago, bottling continues to take place here, evidenced by the huge stainless steel vats in the back room. The wonderful extra virgin oil is a staple in most local homes, but if that's your only reason for visiting, you're missing half the fun. First, add your own business card to the hundreds already plastered on the wall next to the cheese, where you'll find fresh buffalo mozzarella the size of a softball. In the main room, the old stone wheel crusher and hydraulic press are now used as display areas. Check out the dozens of infused vinegars, unusual dried pastas (e.g. grape bunch design), bags of polenta, bins of dried mushrooms, stuffed olives, countless types of biscotti, imported boxed cakes, salame, coppa and prosciutto--it's all right here.

OPEN DAILY

HOURS:
8am-7:30pm

Small Picnic Area

No Credit Cards

Owners:
Lucchesi & Particelli
Families

Not only is the olive oil excellent, it's a bargain: $7.50 for sixteen ounces and $30 for a 3-liter jug. They'll ship anywhere. You gotta love this place!

SUNSHINE FOODS
1117 Main Street • St. Helena • (707) 963-7070

DELI • GROCERY • BAKERY • WINES

OPEN DAILY

SUMMER HOURS:
7:30am-9pm

WINTER HOURS:
7:30am-8pm

V, MC

Sunshine Market should be a case study for the Harvard Business School. This little market has been in St. Helena for generations and could easily have gone the way of most neighborhood grocers when the big guys came to town. Instead, *Sunshine* successfully reinvented itself. Organic produce, gourmet cheeses, smoked fish, artisan breads, specialty foods, a deli, fresh meats and a fish market make this a great place to shop. Custom sandwiches from the deli are very good, salads are outstanding (e.g. mango and cucumber or cous cous and raisin), hot and cold entrées and side dishes are ideal for takeout. A good part of *Sunshine's* success can be attributed to their commitment to finding and featuring high-quality local food purveyors who are often on hand offering samples. *Sweetie Pies* and *Sweet Finale* are responsible for the decadent desserts, and *Kikka Sushi Company* comes in daily to make fresh sushi and sashimi. *Sunshine* has an excellent selection of Napa wines; many are chilled and ready to go.

Kikka Sushi makes party platters to order, ranging from $20 for a 54-piece vegetarian selection to $100 for the super deluxe sushi and sashimi. Order a day in advance.

MODEL BAKERY
1357 Main Street • St. Helena • (707) 963-8192

BAKERY • ESPRESSO • CAFÉ

Model has been a favorite place for locals to meet over muffins and coffee (or lattes) for nearly twenty years. Every morning the countertops and display cases are overflowing with muffins, scones, croissants, and pastries, replaced by cookies, brownies, and lemon bars in the afternoon. Several freshly made soup, salad and sandwich specials are offered at lunchtime, along with a fantastic oven-fired pizza-of-the-day, by the slice. *Model* is particularly well known for its specialty breads. Two daily specials are offered alongside their signature breads of sourdough, sweet French, walnut honey, wheat, and ciabatta. The starter for the popular sourdough bread originated from Napa Valley wine grapes many years ago. No slouch in the dessert department, *Model's* beautiful cakes, pies, tarts, and pastries are delicious and can be made to order. Indoor seating is limited to just a few tables.

CLOSED MONDAYS

HOURS:
Tu-Sa: 7am-6pm
Su: 8am-4pm

LUNCH:
11am until gone!

Pizza

Espresso

No Credit Cards

Owner:
Karen Mitchell

ST. HELENA

At lunchtime, Model's oven-fired pizza with its thin, crisp crust is highly recommended at $4 a slice. Check out the chalk board for the daily special. Go early, because it goes fast.

29 JOE'S
677 St. Helena Hwy • St. Helena • (707) 967-0820

ESPRESSO • COFFEE HOUSE • DRIVE-THRU

OPEN DAILY

HOURS:
M-F: 5:30am-5pm
Sa: 6:30am-3:30pm
Su: 7:30am-3:30pm

No Credit Cards

Located on the southern outskirts of town, *29 Joe's* is worth mentioning not only for the consistently good espresso drinks, but also for two other very important reasons. First and foremost, in addition to inside seating, there is, wonder of wonders, a DRIVE-THRU option! This is the *only* drive-through north of Napa. The second, equally important reason is Joe's hours of operation. If you're desperate for a latte early in the morning, this is the one and only place in St. Helena that opens before 7am. On weekdays, you can roll through Joe's in your bathrobe and slippers as early as 5:30am (in which case the drive-thru is highly recommended), 6:30am Saturday, and 7:30am Sunday. Fresh muffins, scones, morning buns, and pastries are delivered daily. When the weather is nice, there is a very pleasant patio area out back with views of the mountains. *Dean & DeLuca* is located across the parking lot, and V Sattui is across the street.

 Joe's is not obvious from the road. It's located behind the Flora Springs Tasting Room and shares a parking lot with Dean & DeLuca. If frequent trips are planned, ask for the coffee card.

NAPA VALLEY COFFEE ROASTING CO.
1400 Oak Avenue • St. Helena • (707) 963-4491

ESPRESSO • COFFEE BEANS • GIFTS

This neighborhood coffee house is a favorite gathering place for locals. Gourmet coffees, espressos, lattes, and frappés are house specialties. They do all their own bean roasting here. Check the board behind the counter, and you'll see a long list of custom blends done for many of area's best restaurants. Buy one of these or design your own. There is plenty of seating inside, and a few bistro tables streetside for catching a few rays or people watching. In the morning, fresh orange juice, muffins, bagels, and pastries are available, replaced by cookies, brownies and other sweets in the afternoon. A delightful gift shop occupies the center of the room with an ever-changing inventory. Books, pottery, table linens, hats and great-looking T-shirts all make fun gifts. Check out the local magazines in the bookcase as well as the bulletin board for activities taking place throughout the valley.

OPEN DAILY

HOURS:
7:30am-6pm

V, MC (Over $5)

Ask for a Cupper's Club card to start accruing credits for a free gourmet coffee. A separate card is offered for whole bean purchases.

THE BIG DIPPER
1336 Oak Avenue • St. Helena • (707) 963-2616

ICE CREAM • SMOOTHIES

CLOSED SUNDAYS

HOURS:
M-F: 11:30am-6pm
Sa: 11:30am-5pm

No Credit Cards

St. Helena's local ice cream parlor isn't located on Main Street; it's one block west on Oak Avenue across the street from the Catholic school. Is that every kid's dream or what? Filled with American memorabilia that includes a mint-condition Wurlitzer jukebox, posters, signs, and even an antique ice cream scoop collection, *The Big Dipper* is a tiny "blast from the past" well worth the detour off Main Street. Choose from over a dozen flavors of wonderfully rich ice cream made by Peninsula Creamery in Palo Alto. When you a order a single scoop here, you get your money's worth. More to the point, where else can you still get an ice cream cone for only $1.75 a scoop? Believe it or not, this is the only place in town you can get a smoothie (made with ice cream, of course). *The Big Dipper* also has Hawaiian Shave Ice. You won't find the exotic fresh-fruit flavors you get in Hawaii, but they're still pretty tasty and very effective in conjuring up images of grass skirts and sandy beaches.

St. Helena has an annual Hometown Harvest Festival at the end of October featuring foods, crafts, and the highlight, a Pet Parade with awards for best costume.

ADVENTURES IN DINING

ST. HELENA FARMERS MARKET
Crane Park • St. Helena

FARMERS MARKET • CAFE • PICNIC AREA

Every Friday morning from May through October, the *St. Helena Farmers Market* is an impossibly perfect slice of Wine Country living. Located at the base of the western hills on a country road flanked by vineyards, it's nothing short of a picture-postcard setting. Locals make the *Farmers Market* a weekly ritual, as much for the socializing as for the incredible selection of fresh fruit, vegetables, and flowers. Specialty vendors sell everything from infused oils and vinegars to smoked salmon and hummus. Local craftsman and artisans display jewelry, birdhouses, pottery, garden ornaments and much more. Head to the café for coffee or a latte, treat yourself to a freshly baked pastry, and enjoy performances by a classical guitarist or balladeer. Go early, and you'll be rubbing elbows with the white-jacketed students from the CIA or the Napa Valley College Culinary School. Go late, and you may find some last-minute bargains as vendors lighten the load to take home.

SEASONAL
MAY-OCTOBER
Friday Mornings
7:30am-11:30am

Espresso

Crafts

Flowers

Specialty Foods

Crane Park is one of our recommended picnic spots. Bring your own bocce balls, and you can use one of the immaculate courts any time city leagues aren't playing.

FARMERS MARKETS & ROADSIDE STANDS
Silverado Trail at Deer Park • St. Helena

PEACHES • STRAWBERRIES • PRODUCE

ST. HELENA

ROADSIDE STAND
SEASONAL
JUNE-JULY

Peaches only

DEER PARK NORTHWEST CORNER

This roadside stand sells peaches, peaches, and only peaches grown in the neighboring orchards. The season usually starts in June and continues for 6-8 weeks. Ask for a sample, and if you want to eat them immediately, we recommend getting help in selecting ones that are suitably ripe. Most are best if allowed to ripen for a day or two. Delicious!

ROADSIDE STAND
SEASONAL
MAY-NOVEMBER

Strawberries
Peaches

Fruits
Vegetables
Pumpkins

DEER PARK SOUTHWEST CORNER

Open May through November, this roadside stand carries a huge variety of high-quality fruits and vegetables. Everything is grown locally or nearby (quite a lot comes from Lodi). The season starts with locally grown strawberries, usually available for a couple of months, and then moves on to peaches, kiwis, tomatoes, peppers, sweet corn, cantaloupe, watermelon, squash, and much more. In October, it's a good spot for pumpkins, gourds and Indian corn.

Making strawberry jam? They usually have a few flats of very ripe berries expressly for that purpose, so ask!

TOP ST. HELENA PICNIC SPOTS
WHEN AT A WINERY, BUY WINE FROM YOUR HOST

L. MARTINI WINERY • CRANE PARK • LYMAN PARK

LOUIS MARTINI WINERY, located on Hwy 29 on the southern end of St. Helena, has a nice little park just to the left of the Tasting Room entrance. There are no views, but this shady picnic grove is quite pleasant, situated behind the historic, ivy-covered winery. It's private and surprisingly quiet, given its close proximity to Hwy 29.

LOUIS MARTINI WINERY

Open Daily
10am-4:30pm
254 St Helena Hwy S.
(707) 963-2736

CRANE PARK is surrounded by vineyards and has spectacular views of the western hills. It is also home to the *St. Helena Farmers Market*. It doesn't get a whole lot better than this! Tennis and bocce ball courts may be used at no cost. The easiest way to get there is to take White Sulphur Springs to Crane Avenue.

CRANE PARK

Open Daily
On Crane Avenue
between Grayson
& White Sulphur
Springs Rd.

LYMAN PARK is right out of a Norman Rockwell painting, complete with fountain and gazebo. Located on Main Street across from the Post Office, it's a pleasant place to relax on a hot summer's day. It is also a popular "bag-lunch" spot for locals and visitors.

LYMAN PARK

Open Daily
On Main Street,
between Adams and
Madrona.

The St. Helena Chamber of Commerce sponsors half a dozen free evening Concerts in the Park (Lyman Park) in June and July. Bring a picnic and enjoy the show! (707) 963-4456.

TOP ST. HELENA PICNIC SITES
PICNIC ETIQUETTE: CHECK IN WITH THE TASTING ROOM

FOLIE À DEUX WINERY • LEDUCQ VINEYARDS

FOLIE À DEUX

Open Daily
10am-5:30pm
3070 N. St. Helena Hwy
(707) 963-1160

Tasting fee: $5
Bottles start at $12

FOLIE À DEUX WINERY certainly knows how to make an entrance. A couple of years ago, a long, curved driveway was carved through the vineyards, ending in front of *Folie à Deux's* restored, turn-of-the-century Victorian farmhouse, the focal point of the property. The picnic tables are right in front, perfectly situated to enjoy a 360-degree view of the surrounding vineyards and hills.

LEDUCQ VINEYARDS

Open Daily
Wed-Sun 10am-5pm
3222 Ehlers Lane
(707) 963-5972

Tasting fee: $5
refundable with
purchase

Bottles start at $19

LEDUCQ VINEYARDS is a very fine example of a "ghost winery," located on one the prettiest country lanes in Napa Valley. The rustic stone structure was built in 1886 by German immigrant and winemaker Bernard Ehlers. Prohibition halted production, and the property changed hands numerous times over the years. French businessman Jean Leducq founded the current business in 1989 and bought the historic winery building in 2000. The wonderful picnic area is like a private park. It's beautifully landscaped with a fountain & shade trees, but no tables, so bring a blanket. You'll get a magical view of Napa Valley few people see.

Right on the other side of Hwy 29 you'll find the St. Helena Premium Outlet Stores including Coach, Donna Karan, Brooks Brothers, and Jones New York.

ST. HELENA NITE LIFE

1351 LOUNGE

The 1351 LOUNGE is a fantastic addition to the Valley's nite life scene. The closest thing you'll get to food here are the olives in your drink, but that's the point: St .Helena has no shortage of fine dining establishments, but a bar or "lounge" of this caliber is hard to find. Cocktails are outstanding and LARGE. Everything is fresh squeezed and no pre-packaged mixes are ever used. The "industrial chic" look is very hip and uncluttered: cement floors, black and chrome tables and chairs, black leather banquettes, dim lighting; you get the picture. Check out the huge bank vault door at the end of the room.

1351 is also one of the best places in the valley for live music every Thursday through Saturday. On Thursday, there's typically a solo performer, and on weekends, live bands perform. Owners Paul and Sayle know the SF music scene well and have been booking high-end blues and R&B artists you'd normally have to drive into the city to hear. AND, when things get hopping, there's dancing! Who knew St. Helena could be so exciting?

1351 LOUNGE
1351 Main Street
(707) 963-1969
Open Daily 5pm-2am

Live Music Th-Sa:
9:30pm-1:30am

No cover Thursday
$5 cover Fri & Sa

1351 does special Halloween and New Year's Eve parties, complete with decorations, DJ, and dancing. It's a good idea to reserve a space in advance.

ST. HELENA NITE LIFE

ANA'S CANTINA • SILVERADO BREWING CO.

ANA'S CANTINA
1205 Main Street
(707) 963-4921
Hours: 11am-2am
Karaoke Thursday:
9pm-1am
Live Music Fri-Sat:
9:30pm-1:30am
No cover

ANA'S CANTINA is a local bar that looks and feels like it's been around forever, and it has! There's nothing fancy here, but on the weekends when there's a live band or a DJ, the place is hoppin'. Ana's serves lunch daily, primarily Mexican selections. Rumor has it Karoke Night on Thursdays is a hoot.

SILVERADO BREWING
3020 St. Helena Hwy
(707) 967-9876

Bar Hours:
Su-Th: 4:30pm-12am
F-Sa: 11:30am-12am

Live Music Th-Sat:
9:30pm-Midnight
No cover

SILVERADO BREWING COMPANY There's live music every Friday and Saturday night in the bar at *Silverado Brewing Company*. Local bands are featured, playing everything from rock to jazz. The bar stays open until midnight on weekends, but food is only served until 10pm.

Hurd's Beeswax Candle Factory, which used to be located next door to Silverado Brewing Company, has moved to Calistoga, next to Galleria del Arte.

ST. HELENA NITE LIFE

THE WHITE BARN • CAMEO CINEMA

THE WHITE BARN, located at the end of a charming country lane, is really an 1872 Carriage House turned 85-seat performing arts hall. Founded in 1985 by Nancy Garden as a means of bringing cultural events to the upper valley, programming is wonderfully eclectic, including musical revues, cabaret, readings, the occasional theatrical event, and in August, a classic film festival. *The White Barn* is authentically rustic and low-tech, with original wood floors, and *very* creaky stairs leading up to the performance loft (so don't even think about sneaking out undetected!). There's usually something going on at *The White Barn* one weekend every month, with the exception of June, July and December. Ticket prices typically range from $20-$40. To receive a schedule, call the box office at (707) 963-7002.

THE WHITE BARN
2727 White Sulphur Springs Avenue

For schedule info:
(707) 963-7002

The CAMEO CINEMA is a local treasure. Single-screen movie houses may have gone the way of dinosaurs, but not in St. Helena! This lovingly restored jewelbox even has old-fashioned love seats in the back. It's also a bargain. Don't miss it!

CAMEO CINEMA
1340 Main Street
(707) 963-9779
Adults: $6.75
Seniors: $3.50

Every performance at The White Barn benefits a designated organization, such as local youth and school groups, music programs, The Red Cross, the NV Symphony, and many more!

Notes

Calistoga

Calistoga Inn Restaurant & Brewery

Calistoga

Carefully restored buildings from the past add an old-fashioned charm to this city at the north end of the Napa Valley. Known for its mud baths and mineral waters, Calistoga is the epitome of small-town living.

It was founded in the mid 1800's by Sam Brannan, the leader of a Morman expedition that landed in San Francisco. After the discovery of gold in Sacramento, Brannan became California's first millionaire, and he used his wealth to develop this area using Saratoga, New York, as his template. He opened the first spa in Calistoga in 1862. A few years later, the residential and commercial areas were developed, and the railroad to Calistoga was completed. By the 1880's Calistoga had become a resort destination and a center for agriculture and viticulture. Although the railroad is gone, the tourism trade still thrives. For a historical perspective in three dimensions, be sure to visit the Sharpsteen Museum with its magnificent diorama, restored 19th century cottage, and other exhibits located one block off Lincoln Avenue on Washington Street.

With over 15 fine restaurants today, Calistoga far surpasses expectations normally held for cities with a population of only 5,500 people. The downtown area revolves around Lincoln Avenue. Walking along its four blocks you will not find any chain stores or fast food establishments here. Instead look for small boutiques, art galleries, a local museum, spas, inns, bookstores, and of course, the restaurants, delis and bakeries. Believe it or not, there is late-night dining and live music at a couple of restaurants.

There are also three small but sophisticated wine shops carrying the best vintages of the Napa Valley as well as imported gems from Europe. Be sure to visit Carlo Marchiori's gallery displaying his unbelievable artistic skills as a master of trompe l'oeil. Better yet, come on Saturday and take a tour of his home, which is the ultimate example of how to "fool the eye" with paint and plaster. If hiking is more to your liking, pretend you are Robert Louis Stevenson and hike up Mount St. Helena and rest in his old home. You can even play a game of golf or tennis at the public facilities within walking distance of Lincoln Avenue.

With a large selection of bed-and-breakfasts to ensure a good night's sleep, feel free to tour the world-renowned wineries, pamper yourself at one of the many spas, or take a long bike ride through the vineyards. At the end of the day, you will agree this friendly village is a haven for locals and tourists alike.

CALISTOGA KEY

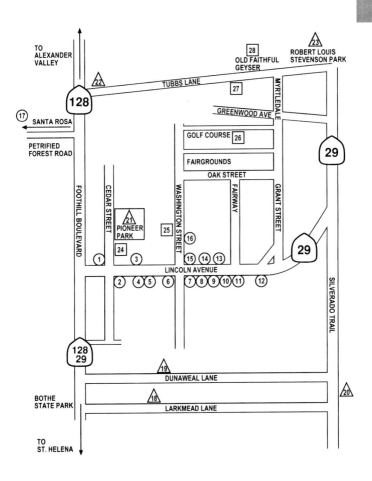

TO
ALEXANDER
VALLEY

28
OLD FAITHFUL
GEYSER

23
ROBERT LOUIS
STEVENSON PARK

22
TUBBS LANE

27

128

17
SANTA ROSA

GREENWOOD AVE

PETRIFIED
FOREST ROAD

GOLF COURSE 26

29

FAIRGROUNDS

OAK STREET

21
PIONEER
PARK

25

24

1

3

16

15 14 13

LINCOLN AVENUE

2 4 5 6   7 8 9 10 11   12

29

128
29

19
DUNAWEAL LANE

BOTHE
STATE PARK

18
LARKMEAD LANE

20

TO
ST. HELENA

CEDAR STREET
WASHINGTON STREET
FAIRWAY
MYRTLEDALE
GRANT STREET
FOOTHILL BOULEVARD
SILVERADO TRAIL

Notes

ALL SEASONS
1400 Lincoln Avenue • Calistoga • (707) 942-9111

CALIFORNIA

All Seasons celebrates its 20th anniversary in 2003, and its successful longevity speaks volumes. Locals love the place not only for its cozy ambience and moderate prices, but for the consistently fine food. The menu features elegant and creative salads, vegetarian pastas, and heartier dishes like rack of lamb, pork chops, braised beef ribs, duck confit and grilled salmon. The added bonus of a spectacular and well-hidden wine shop on the premises makes *All Seasons* unique and a favorite place to bring friends when we want to show them the "real" wine country. Chef Kevin Kathman and sommelier Sean Meyer take the of pairing of food and wine very seriously. They'll happily offer assistance in navigating the wine list, BUT...you can also ask for their help in choosing a bottle from the fabulous wine shop tucked away in a back room. This is not only great fun, but you'll get the wine at retail prices and pay only a nominal corkage fee. Notable boutique wines from France as well as the Napa and Sonoma Valleys are house specialties.

OPEN DAILY

LUNCH: Noon-3pm
DINNER:
6pm-9:30pm

Appetizers: $6-$15
Entrées: $16-$24
Desserts: $6-$7

Wine Shop

Wine Bar
Winning Wine List
Corkage: $15
Reservations: Yes

V, MC
Locals' Favorite
Special Events
Catering
Takeout

Chef: Kevin Kathman

The All Seasons Wine Shop specializes in boutique wines from California and around the world. They can ship to most states. Their website is www.allseasonswineshop.com.

CALISTOGA

BOSKO'S TRATTORIA
1364 Lincoln Avenue • Calistoga • (707) 942-9088

ITALIAN

OPEN DAILY

LUNCH: 11am-4pm
Appetizers: $3-$6
Entrées: $4-$11
Desserts: $3-$4

DINNER: 4pm-10pm
Appetizers: $3-$6
Entrées: $11-$14
Desserts: $4-$5

Pizza
Continuous Dining
Late Kitchen
Corkage: $5
Reservations: No

V, MC

Locals' Favorite
Family Friendly
Takeout

Located in a beautiful sandstone building built in the late 1880's, *Bosko's* is a pleasant, no-frills spot to have a hearty Italian meal at very reasonable prices. The wood-burning oven turns out Italian-style pizzas and calzone, and delicious handmade pasta is served with creative and traditional sauces. Generous salads and foccacia sandwiches are good choices at lunchtime, and there are always a few combination specials that are a particularly good value: any pasta with soup or salad for $9.95 or half a sandwich with soup or salad for $6.95. Tasty Italian desserts and espresso will complete your meal in fine trattoria style.

Wine and beer are available by the glass, or choose a bottle from a limited but reasonably priced selection on the shelf at retail prices. There is no corkage fee if purchased on site.

Bosko's is one of Calistoga's best choices for family-friendly dining. The pizza is very good and the traditional pasta dishes will please most picky eaters.

BRANNAN'S GRILL

1374 Lincoln Avenue • Calistoga • (707) 942-2233

AMERICAN

Opened in March of 1998, this beautifully designed and appointed restaurant has become a favorite of both locals and tourists. The ambience is cozy and comfortable with original wall murals by Carlo Marchiori, a large river-rock fireplace, many booths, and a solid mahogany bar, circa 1880. A unique window system opens fully, creating the feel of a sidewalk café, perfect for warm-weather days. The luncheon menu features creative salads and sandwiches like the Duck and Nectarine Spinach Salad and the Fried Green Tomato BLT. The hamburger with caramelized onions, cheddar and bacon is a treat! In the evening, serious comfort food like pork loin, beef tenderloin, hangar steak, and the house specialty, Lamb Steak Frites, (garlic and herb rubbed lamb sirloin with fries) take center stage. The mashed potatoes are heavenly! Full bar service includes a nice wine list, 15-20 wines by the glass, 25-30 half-bottles, and locally produced premium microbrews. Many say this is the place for the best Martini in the Valley!

OPEN DAILY

LUNCH:
11:30am-3pm
Sa: 11:30am-3:30pm
Appetizers: $8-$12
Entrées: $10-$19
Desserts: $8

DINNER:
4:30pm-9pm
Sa: 4:30pm-9:30pm
Appetizers: $8-$12
Entrées: $17-$29
Desserts: $8

Wine Bar
Corkage: $15
Reservations: Yes

V, MC
Special Events
Catering
Takeout
Chef: Steve Atkins

Notice the quality and detail of this beautifully restored building. The wonderful wall murals were created by local resident and internationally renowned trompe l'oeil painter, Carlo Marchiori.

CALISTOGA

CAFÉ SARAFORNIA
1413 Lincoln Avenue • Calistoga • (707) 942-0555

AMERICAN

OPEN DAILY

HOURS: 7am-3pm

BREAKFAST:
7am-3pm
Prices: $5-$11

LUNCH: Noon-3pm
Prices: $6-$11
Desserts: $3-$5

Hamburgers
Continuous Dining
Corkage: None
Reservations: No

V, MC
Locals' Favorite
Family Friendly
Takeout

Combining California and Saratoga, founding father Sam Brannan came up with the name "Calistoga." He also called it "Sarafornia" one night after one too many drinks, thus the name for this small café that is the morning meeting place for locals. Quick, simple and tasty breakfasts are served all day at small tables, booths, and around the U-shaped counter. Huevos Rancheros, a house specialty, becomes even more satisfying with a cup of espresso or a Mimosa! Parents will appreciate the special Kid's Breakfast including beverage for $4.25. The luncheon fare is hearty, with 1/3 pound hamburgers, large entrée salads, and a signature wrap sandwich called the Jalisco Club. And if fire-breathing chili is your thing, you've met your match. They only offer "red" or "white" wine by the glass so feel free to bring a bottle; there's no corkage fee, just add a couple bucks to the tip instead. The windows open onto the street and are a great place to watch the world go by on a sunny day. Moderate prices guarantee a return visit.

Be sure to check out the 3-D mural on the wall inside. And don't forget to try the homemade pancakes or French toast with orange butter!

CALISTOGA INN RESTAURANT & BREWERY
1250 Lincoln Avenue • Calistoga • (707) 942-4101

AMERICAN

Located on the bank of the Napa River in downtown Calistoga, this small inn (18 rooms) with its own restaurant and brewery has a charming, European appearance that wouldn't be out of place in the Italian Lake District or the Bavarian Alps. A large, wisteria-shaded patio is perfect for casual, alfresco dining. Inside, the restaurant is more formal and provides seating for 110 diners. Salads are a meal in themselves, and sandwiches come with delicious garlic cheese fries. House specialties include burgers, meats, chicken and fresh fish cooked on the outdoor wood-fired grill. Not surprisingly, everything on the menu, especially those yummy garlic cheese fries, pairs nicely with the award-winning beer made in the micro-brewery adjacent to the patio. Brunch is served Saturday and Sunday from 10am-3pm. A large bar provides a pub-like atmosphere, featuring live music (mostly blues, country, or jazz) every Friday and Saturday night from 8:30pm-11pm.

OPEN DAILY
LUNCH:
11:30am-3pm
Prices: $5-$14
DINNER:
5:30pm-9:30pm
Appetizers: $5-$13
Entrées: $14-$24
Desserts: $4-$6

Hamburgers
Brewpub
Brunch (Sat & Sun)
Continuous Dining
Corkage: $10
Reservations: Yes

V, MC, AE
Nite Life
Family Friendly
Special Events
Takeout

Chef:
Rosie Dunsford

This is the best place in town to enjoy lunch with a cold beer on a hot summer's day! Enjoy live music in the Courtyard, on Sundays from 3pm-6pm, May-October.

CATAHOULA RESTAURANT & SALOON
1457 Lincoln Avenue • Calistoga • (707) 942-2275

AMERICAN

CLOSED TUESDAYS

DINNER:
5:30pm-10:30pm
Appetizers: $5-$8
Entrées: $17-$23
Desserts: $5-$7

Pizza
Late Kitchen
Corkage: $8.50
Reservations: Yes

V, MC
Family Friendly
Special Events
Catering
Takeout

Chef: Jan Birnbaum

If you want comfort food with spice, this is the place for you. The flavors are intense and robust just like the Master Chef/Owner Jan Birnbaum, a native of Louisiana, who trained with Paul Prudhomme. Think gumbo, andouille sausage, red eye gravy, catfish, grits, and mix them with the expertise of one who was also the head chef of the five-star *Quilted Giraffe Restaurant* in New York City. After serving as the Executive Chef at the *Campton Place Hotel Restaurant* in San Francisco for five years, he settled in Calistoga in 1994. The result is a delightful, creative meal most often cooked in the wood-burning oven. Not only does it produce whole roasted fish, but fabulous pizzas as well. Grilled steaks, salmon, and vegetables have that unmistakable Louisiana flavor with a Napa Valley flair, utilizing the freshest of local produce. Check to see if Chef Jan is actually going to be there–the food seems to be better when he's in the kitchen.

Call for Catahoula's schedule of special holiday events and cooking classes. And in case you're wondering: The Catahoula is the official hound dog of the state of Louisiana!

CHECKERS RESTAURANT
1414 Lincoln Avenue • Calistoga • (707) 942-9300

ITALIAN

Good food is easy to find in this upscale yet casual eatery. Although the decor has been updated in the last six months to provide a calmer atmosphere for the diner, the sense of whimsy continues. Instead of art hanging from the ceiling, art deco now hangs on the walls. This combination is not surprising when you realize that *Checkers*, *Brannan's* and *Flatiron Grill* are all owned by Mark Young and Ron Goldin, masters of good taste in food and decor. Pizzas and pastas are the main event here, and entrée -size salads are perfect luncheon fare. The focaccia sandwiches, which include soup or salad of the day, are hearty enough for the biggest appetites. New chef, Adriane Olea, continues to add a touch of Thai to the pizza toppings as well as the delicious Oriental salad, both of which have been favorites with the locals! The rest of the menu remains a treat for those looking for more traditional Italian flavors such as linguini carbonara. Desserts are homestyle featuring chocolate or fruit, and the gelato always goes well with the espresso.

Open Daily

LUNCH:
11:30am-3pm
DINNER: 3pm-9pm

Sandwiches: $8-$9
Entrées: $7-$15
Desserts: $3-$5

Pizza

Continuous Dining
Corkage: $10
Reservations: No

V, MC
Locals' Favorite
Family Friendly
Special Events
Catering
Takeout

Chef:
Adriane Olea

For those in a hurry, Checkers has a beautiful wine bar where you can grab a bite to eat and have a nice glass of wine.

FLATIRON GRILL
1440 Lincoln Avenue • Calistoga • (707) 942-1220

AMERICAN

OPEN DAILY

LUNCH:
11:30am-3pm
Prices: $9-$15
Desserts: $4-$5

DINNER:
5:30pm-10pm
Appetizers: $4-$9
Entrées: $13-$17
Desserts: $5

Hamburgers
Wine Bar
Corkage: $10
Reservations: Yes

V, MC
Locals' Favorite
Special Events
Catering
Takeout

Chef: Steve Atkins

If you are looking for casual dining in an upscale atmosphere, this newly opened restaurant is the perfect choice. Totally remodeled inside since its days as *Cin Cin*, the tobacco-colored walls, dimmed lighting, suede covered booths, and beautiful wood floors create a cozy, understated elegance that fits perfectly with the comfort food on the menu. A gorgeous, dark wood wine bar separates two distinct dining areas. The collection of cow paintings by local artist Lowell Herrero hanging on the walls adds a nice, whimsical touch. Top-quality dining at reasonable prices is the goal of Executive Chef Steve Atkins. He achieves that by carefully preparing each person's order as requested and serves it with simple elegance. Shrimp cocktail, onion rings, French fries, grilled steak and salmon, roasted chicken, macaroni and cheese, potatoes au gratin, and other old fashioned delights are a rare and welcome sight these days–who said you can't go home again? The extensive wine list is an added attraction.

Early Bird Alert: Receive a complete dinner for the price of a single entrée 4:30pm-6:00pm daily!

CALISTOGA

HYDRO BAR & GRILL
1403 Lincoln Avenue • Calistoga • (707) 942-9777

AMERICAN

Hydro can be best described as "bar" first, "grill" second. It is THE late-night spot in Calistoga. Casual is the operative word here: enter through the large double doors, help yourself to a menu, and find a table. Nothing is pretentious, just brick walls, solid wooden tables, and hardwood floors. The food is equally uncomplicated and just the thing when you're looking for a no-frills meal. Breakfast features all the usual favorites and is very popular on weekends. Burgers, sandwiches, soups and salads are offered at lunchtime. Add a few simple entrées and you've got the dinner menu, which is served until 11pm, and midnight on weekends.

Hydro is owned by Alex Dierkhising of *All Seasons* restaurant across the street. This is a great spot to kick back, order a beer, and enjoy the music. The bar is open until midnight on weekdays, 2am weekends.

OPEN DAILY
BREAKFAST:
8:30am-11:30am
Prices: $3-$7

LUNCH:
11:30am-4pm
Prices: $7-$16

DINNER: 4pm-11pm
Appetizers: $7-$8
Entrées: $13-$20
Desserts: $5

Hamburgers
Continuous Dining
Late Kitchen
Corkage: $10
Reservations: No

V, MC
Nite Life
Takeout

Hydro is the only restaurant north of Yountville serving a full menu past 11:00pm, a rarity among Napa Valley restaurants.

PACIFICO
1237 Lincoln Avenue • Calistoga • (707) 942-4400

MEXICAN

OPEN DAILY
11am-10pm
BRUNCH:
Sa-Su: 11am-3pm

Appetizers: $3-$6
Entrées: $7-$14
Desserts: $4-$5

Continuous Dining
Excellent Beer List
Corkage: $7

Reservations: No
(unless 7 or more)

V, MC
Locals' Favorite
Family Friendly
Special Events
Takeout

Chef:
Salvador Gomez

Several years ago, Chef Salvador Gomez traveled throughout Mexico intent on bringing back authentic recipes from his homeland. He succeeded. His menu includes creative interpretations of centuries-old Mexican recipes, as well as updated versions of traditional favorites. Fresh, vibrant flavors characterize everything on the menu, from the grilled red snapper and ceviche, to the tamales and carnitas tacos. The carnitas tacos are the best we've ever tasted! French doors, casement windows, tile floors, oak tables, ladderback chairs and colorful accents throughout make this a most attractive restaurant. Full menu service is also available in the separate, large bar, equipped with several TVs. The bar has an excellent selection of tap and bottled beers, and over 55 brands of tequila. Needless to say, delicious hand-shaken margaritas are a house specialty. Brunch, served Saturday and Sunday from 10am to 3pm, puts a south-of-the-border twist on any egg dish you desire. Try *Pacifico's* version of Eggs Benedict!

Pacifico is a happening place for locals during happy hour from 4:30pm to 6:00pm, Monday through Friday.

SOO YUAN

1354 Lincoln Avenue • Calisotga • (707) 942-9404

CHINESE

Tucked among several small and narrow storefronts, this little restaurant is easy to pass by. But those in the know have voted this the best place for Chinese dining year after year. The menu is large and contains all of your favorites, plus specialties such as Seafood in Bird Nest, General Chicken, and Imperial Fire Pot. Barely wider than the doorway, the cozy dining room is nothing fancy, with the kitchen at the back and minimal Chinese decoration. Smells of sweet and sour sauce, Kung Pao chicken and hot jasmine tea greet you at the front door. The service is friendly and efficient. Like most Chinese restaurants, this one does a bustling takeout business as evidenced by the bags lined up by the cash register. Delivery is available in Calistoga for orders over $15 plus a 10% charge. They will also deliver to St. Helena for orders over $30 plus a 15% delivery charge.

OPEN DAILY

LUNCH:
11:30am-2:30pm
Appetizers: $3-$4
Entrées: $6-$7

DINNER:
2:30pm-10pm
Appetizers: $3-$4
Entrées: $6-$12

Continuous Dining
Corkage: $5

Reservations: No
(unless 5 or more)

V, MC, AE, DC
Locals' Favorite
Family Friendly
Special Events
Catering
Takeout

Too tired to go out? They deliver! Enjoy a complete Chinese dinner delivered direct to your door or stop by and pick it up. Delivery area includes Calistoga and St. Helena!

TRIPLE S RANCH
4600 Mountain Ranch Rd • Calistoga • (707) 942-6730

AMERICAN

OPEN 4/1-12/31

DINNER:
5pm-9pm
Appetizers: $4-$9
Dinners: $13-$19

Corkage: $5.50

Reservations: Yes

V, MC, AE, DC

Locals' Favorite

Family Friendly

Special Events

Located in the Mayacamas Mountains above Calistoga, the *Triple S Ranch* is a blast from the past. Little, if anything, has been updated since this old barn was converted into a restaurant back in 1960. If you're not wearing jeans, you're probably over dressed. Locals love it for just that reason, along with the great steaks and famous onion rings. Dinner prices include a relish plate, soup or salad, beverage and dessert. Saturday is Prime Rib Night. How 1960's is that? Have a cocktail in the bar, where they still use those tiny bar glasses (which is probably a good idea given that drive in), or sit on the deck and enjoy the sunset. Getting to *Triple S* takes a bit of effort. It's two miles up Petrified Forest Road from the Hwy 128 intersection, then turn right on Home Mountain Ranch Road. At that point you keep going (a mile or so) until you reach *Triple S*. Pay attention to several forks in the road on the way in, so you won't take a wrong turn on the way out in the dark (experience talking). *Triple S* also rents a few VERY BASIC cabins for $90 per night!

 Safari West, a remarkable wildlife preserve, is only a few miles past Triple S. See species of African animals including giraffes and cheetahs by jeep. Tours by appt, call 800-616-2695.

ADVENTURES IN DINING

WAPPO BAR & BISTRO
1226 Washington Street • Calistoga • (707) 942-4712

FUSION

Wonderfully unique is the only way to describe *Wappo*. The style of cuisine is far too original and eclectic to warrant a routine classification. The menu is a veritable travelogue, filled with Mediterranean, Asian, Latin American and South American influences. The chefs clearly love creating new dishes and change the menu frequently, but whatever you choose, you can always count on two things: it will be memorable and delicious. At lunchtime, think hearty soups, foccacia sandwiches so full of wonderful ingredients you can barely get your mouth around them, and enormous salads. For dinner, don't be surprised if you see Ecuadorian Braised Pork on the same menu with Tandoori Chicken and Osso Bucco. In warm weather, alfresco dining under the grapevine-covered arbor next to the fountain is a must. The wine list is every bit as sophisticated and unique as the cuisine, concentrating on small producers in Napa, Sonoma, and Alexander Valleys. Many are moderately priced under $30. DO NOT MISS this Napa Valley original!

CLOSED TUESDAYS

LUNCH:
11:30am-2:30pm
Appetizers: $6-$10
Entrées: $10-$14
DINNER:
6pm-9:30pm
Appetizers: $7-$12
Entrées: $13-$22
Desserts: $5-$6

Winning Wine List
Corkage: $10
Reservations: Yes

V, MC, AE
Locals' Favorite
Bay Area Top 100
Special Events
Catering
Takeout

Chefs:
Aaron Bauman
Michelle Matrux

Looking for a great place for a special celebration? Wappo has a charming private building adjacent to the restaurant that can accommodate up to 40 guests.

CALISTOGA

WAPPO TACO
1458 Lincoln Avenue • Calistoga • (707) 942-8165

MEXICAN

CLOSED TUESDAYS
BREAKFAST:
8am-11am
LUNCH/DINNER:
11am-10pm

Moderately Priced
Continuous Dining

Corkage: $10

Reservations: No
(Yes, if 6 or more)

V, MC, AE, DC
Family Friendly

Catering
Takeout

Chef:
Michelle Matrux

If you love to be the first one in your crowd to try a brand new restaurant, here's one that's sure to cause a stir. Michelle Matrux, chef/owner of the marvelous *Wappo Bistro*, is going for another homerun in downtown Calistoga. If all goes according to plan, *Wappo Taco* will open in January of 2003, serving breakfast, lunch and dinner. The inspiration for this new venture sprang from the enthusiastic response to taco dishes Michelle frequently created as daily specials at *Wappo Bistro*. Consequently, a restaurant devoted solely to authentic, regional Mexican food, with tacos at the core, seemed a natural extension of her talents. Baja Fish tacos, Yucatan Style Grouper, Carnitas, red and green salsa, and chiles rellenos are just a few items you'll see on the menu. Moderately priced, *Wappo Taco* is a casual, family- friendly sort of place, with a traditional "hacienda" decor painted rich, warm colors of red, green and avocado. Mexican folk art decorates the walls. Indoor and patio seating are available. A wine and beer license is pending approval.

The Wapoo Indians, attracted by the abundance of natural hot springs and thermal geysers, settled in this area over 8,000 years ago. They called the land "Hot Oven."

CALISTOGA NATURAL

1426 Lincoln Avenue • Calistoga • (707) 942-5822

DELI • CAFÉ • SMOOTHIES • MARKET

Start your day the healthy way with a 16-ounce organic smoothie, an espresso, and a piece of organic toast and jam in this light-filled natural foods store and café. *Calistoga Natural* is definitely the best spot in town for a smoothie; choose from over 15 tasty combinations on the menu, or create your own. Award-winning Alvarado Street Bakery organic breads sold by the loaf are also used to make sandwiches in the deli. Most menu selections are vegetarian, but free-range turkey and chicken find their way into several tasty concoctions. The deli also offers pizza by the slice, soups, black bean chili, frittata, macaroni and cheese, spring rolls and tempeh burgers. Everything is available for takeout, but there is also a small café inside the store. Whatever you decide to eat, it's bound to be healthy. Mother would approve.

OPEN DAILY
M-Sa: 9am-6pm
Su: 10am-5pm

LUNCH
Prices: $4-$6

Espresso

V, MC

Catering

Chef / Owner:
Kelly Barrett

Calistoga's hot springs have been famous for centuries. Health enthusiasts from around the world come for the mineral waters and mud bath treatments.

PALISADES MARKET
1506 Lincoln Avenue • Calistoga • (707) 942-9549

DELI • PRODUCE • WINES • SPECIALTY FOODS

OPEN DAILY

HOURS: 7:30am-7pm

Espresso

Wine Shop

Picnic Area

V, MC, AE

Catering

Palisades Market is Calistoga's version of the Oakville Grocery. It may not look like anything special from the outside, but inside it is extraordinary. Grab a wire shopping basket and just wander around. You'll see exceptional cheeses, breads, olive oils, vinegars, dressings, sea salt, crackers, chutneys, and pastas. Gift items and wonderful things for the cook or the kitchen seem to be displayed everywhere. In the morning, espresso drinks are available along with fabulous freshly baked pastries. The deli counter is outstanding. Many of the items have a Mexican flair; the wraps and burritos are delicious and can easily be shared. A huge selection of prepared salads and creative entrées are available for lunch and dinner. Needless to say, *Palisades* is a perfect spot to do your picnic provisioning. Don't miss the wine section: it's full of local vintages as well as French and Italian imports, many of them small production or hard-to-find labels. The staff is always eager to please, so do ask if you can't find what you want.

With a little notice, a beautiful gift basket can be custom made for that special hostess gift. They ship!

SCHAT'S BAKERY
1353 Lincoln Avenue • Calistoga • (707) 942-0777

BAKERY • CAFÉ • ESPRESSO • GELATO

Owner Jan Schat, already highly regarded as the head baker for the *Il Fornaio* restaurants, became famous when he and three other San Francisco Bay Area bakers won first place in the 1999 international baking competition held in Paris. He now has his own shop in Calistoga, where he bakes his artisan breads and pastries for the local population to enjoy. Be sure to come early to buy your favorites because booming sales to independent groceries tend to deplete the supply rather quickly. A nice little café serves delicious gelato and espresso until 10pm, making *Schat's* a perfect spot for dessert and coffee after dinner at one of Calistoga's many fine restaurants.

CLOSED TUESDAYS

HOURS: 6am-10pm

Espresso

Ice Cream

V, MC, AE, DC

Owner: Jan Schat

During the summer, stop by after dinner on weekends for a gelato and espresso and listen to live music from 7pm to 10pm.

TOP CALISTOGA PICNIC SITES
PICNIC ETIQUETTE: BUY WINE FROM YOUR HOST

FRANK FAMILY VINEYARDS • CLOS PEGASE

FRANK FAMILY VINEYARDS
Open Daily
10am-5pm
1091 Larkmead Lane
(707) 942-0859

Bottles begin at $29

FRANK FAMILY VINEYARDS' massive stone winery, built in 1884, was once owned by local legend and champagne baron Hans Kornell. It is now on the National Register of Historic Places, and sparkling wines are still produced in the original building. Owners Richard Frank and Koerner Rombauer also produce superb still wines including Chardonnay, Zinfandel, Sangiovese, and three Cabernets. Picnic on the beautiful grounds of this historic site located on a quiet lane with magnificent vineyard and mountain views.

CLOS PEGASE
Open Daily
10:30am-5pm
1060 Dunaweal Lane
(707) 942-4981

Tasting fee: $5-$20

Bottles begin at $14

Cheese and other picnic items for sale on site.

CLOS PEGASE WINERY was designed by award-winning architect Michael Graves. As owner Jan Shrem would gladly tell you, this wonderfully unique building's resemblance to a modern temple is no accident, and Bacchus is the patron saint. *Clos Pegase* has quite an interesting art collection, including original *Clos Pegase* wine labels and a wrecking ball attached to the ceiling by a frayed wire! Picnic in a shady area adjacent to the courtyard, with vineyard & mountain views.

The 3rd Saturday of each month, Clos Pegase owner Jan Shrem presents the highly entertaining saga, "A Bacchanalian History of Wine Seen Through 4,000 Years of Art."

CALISTOGA

TOP CALISTOGA PICNIC SITES
PICNIC ETIQUETTE: CHECK IN WITH THE TASTING ROOM

CUVAISON • PIONEER PARK

CUVAISON is French for "fermentation of wine on the grape skins." Since the winery was founded in 1969, you won't find any historic buildings here, but you will find very nice Chardonnay, Pinot Noir, Merlot and Cabernet wines at reasonable prices. Cuvaison produces over 63,000 cases annually, with Chardonnay representing over 65% of total production. The nicely landscaped picnic area is shaded by 350-year-old oak trees and has great views of the surrounding vineyards.

CUVAISON WINERY
Open Daily
10am-5pm
4550 Silverado Trail
(707) 942-6266

Tasting fee: $9

Bottles start at $22

PIONEER PARK - Located in the heart of downtown Calistoga, just a block off Lincoln Avenue, this charming park is a favorite local spot and the site of numerous art shows and other activities throughout the year. Kids will love it here. THE SHARPSTEEN MUSEUM just on the other side of the park on Washington doesn't have a picnic area, but it is well worth your time. The best way to see it is to ask one of the volunteers to show you around--they really know their stuff. This little jewel box of a museum is chock full of local history!

PIONEER PARK
Open Daily
Elm Street, 1 block
north of Lincoln

SHARPSTEEN MUSEUM
Open Daily
11am-4pm
1311 Washington
(707) 942-5911

Villa Ca'Toga, home of renowned trompe l'oeil artist Carlo Marchiori, is in Calistoga. His gallery, Ca'Toga Galleria D'Arte, is just steps away from the park. Ask about villa tours.

CALISTOGA

TOP CALISTOGA PICNIC SITES
PICNIC ETIQUETTE: BUY WINE FROM YOUR HOST

SUMMERS • R. L. STEVENSON STATE PARK

SUMMERS WINERY
Open Daily
10am-5pm
1171 Tubbs Lane
(707) 942-5508

SUMMERS WINERY – Bocce Ball fans may be interested to know that residents of the upper Napa Valley are crazy for the game. Summers Winery hosts the Mt. St. Helena Bocce Club championships each year, and picnickers are welcome to use the court when it's idle. Enjoy an unobstructed view of the Palisades and Mt. St. Helena from the picnic area. Summers Winery is relatively new on the scene (1997), producing Merlot and Charbono.

RLS STATE PARK
Open Daily
On Hwy 29, 8 miles
north of Calistoga
(707) 942-4575

ROBERT LOUIS STEVENSON STATE PARK – How about a picnic at the top of Mt. St. Helena with views of the Pacific Ocean, San Francisco, and the Sierra peaks? Named for the famous author who spent his honeymoon in the area in 1880, this state park is perhaps best known for the strenuous 9-mile round-trip hike to the top of the highest peak around. The best time to make the trek is in spring or fall–forget about summer, it's way too hot. Bring lots of water and plan on spending 5-6 hours.

For more information on Robert Louis Stevenson, visit the Silverado Museum in St Helena located next to the library. It contains over 8,000 items relating to the author.

CALISTOGA NITE LIFE

CALISTOGA INN & BREWERY • HYDRO

CALISTOGA INN & BREWERY features Open Mic Night every Wednesday from 8:30pm to 11pm. On Friday and Saturday live bands perform from 8:30pm-11pm. Most of the groups are local, playing blues, country, jazz or light rock–never anything heavy–there is an inn overhead, after all. On Sunday afternoons during the summer, there's live music on the patio from 3pm-6pm.

CALISTOGA INN
1250 Lincoln Avenue
(707) 942-4101
Open Mic Wed
Live Music Fri & Sat
No Cover

Kitchen closes at
9:30pm

HYDRO BAR & GRILL is the only *really* late night place in Calistoga. Food can be ordered until 11pm daily, and midnight on the weekends. The bar stays open until at least midnight during the week, and 1:30am Friday and Saturday, when live bands perform, beginning at 9:30pm. The music is usually R&B or blues. Every Sunday *"The Swing Seven"* performs from 7pm-10pm.

HYDRO BAR
1403 Lincoln Avenue
(707) 942-9777
Live Music Fri-Sun
No Cover

Bar Closes at 1:30am
Fri & Sat

Bar Closes around
midnight weekdays.

FOR COMPLETE DETAILS ON BOTH OF THESE RESTAURANTS, SEE THE CALISTOGA RESTUARANT SECTION.

Calistoga is famous for its spas thanks to the natural hot springs. During the winter, nearly all the spas offer special deals on various mud treatments, particularly during the week.

Notes

Guide to Index

Index by Category

Alphabetical Listing

Bakeries

Bay Area Top 100

Breakfast

Brewpubs

Catering

Continuous Dining

Delicatessens

Espresso

Family Friendly

Farmers Markets

Full Bar

Hamburgers

Ice Cream

Late Kitchens

Locals' Favorites

Nite Life

Outdoor Dining

Picnic Spots

Pizza

Romantic Spots

Specialty Markets

Special Events

Sunday Brunch

Takeout

Types of Cuisine

American

Asian

California

Chinese

French

Fusion

Indian

Italian

Japanese

Mediterranean